A Guide to Analyzing Your Fashion Industry Internship

Michele Granger

Chair, Fashion Program
Stephens College
Columbia, Missouri

A Guide to Analyzing Your Fashion Industry Internship

Michele Granger

Chair, Fashion Program
Stephens College
Columbia, Missouri

Delmar Publishers

I(T)P An International Thomson Publishing Company

Albany · Bonn · Boston · Cincinnati · Detroit · London · Madrid · Melbourne
Mexico City · New York · Pacific Grove · Paris · San Francisco · Singapore · Tokyo
Toronto · Washington

Cover by Bob Clarke

Delmar Staff

Acquisitions Editor: Christopher Anzalone

Developmental Editor: Jeffrey D. Litton

Project Editor: Eugenia L. Orlandi

Production Coordinator: Douglas J. Hyldelund

Art & Design Coordinator: Jennifer Gaines

COPYRIGHT © 1996
By Delmar Publishers
a division of International Thomson Publishing Inc.

The ITP logo is a trademark under license

Printed in the United States of America

For more information, contact:

Delmar Publishers
3 Columbia Circle, Box 15015
Albany, New York 12212-5015

International Thomson Editores
Campos Eliseos 385, Piso 7
Col Polanco
11560 Mexico D F Mexico

International Thomson Publishing Europe
Berkshire House 168-173
High Holborn
London WC1V7AA
England

International Thomson Publishing GmbH
Königswinterer Strasse 418
53227 Bonn
Germany

Thomas Nelson Australia
102 Dodds Street
South Melbourne, 3205
Victoria, Australia

International Thomson Publishing Asia
221 Henderson Road
#05 - 10 Henderson Building
Singapore 0315

Nelson Canada
1120 Birchmount Road
Scarborough, Ontario
Canada M1K 5G4

International Thomson Publishing - Japan
Hirakawacho Kyowa Building, 3F
2-2-1 Hirakawacho
Chiyoda-ku, Tokyo 102
Japan

All rights reserved. No part of this work covered by the copyright hereon may be reproduced or used in any form or by any means—graphic, electronic, or mechanical, including photocopying, recording, taping, or information storage and retrieval systems—without the written permission of the publisher.

1 2 3 4 5 6 7 8 9 10   XXX   01 00 99 98 97 96 95

Library of Congress Cataloging-in-Publication Data
Granger, Michele
    A guide to analyzing your fashion industry internship / Michele Granger
      p. cm.
    Includes index.
    ISBN 0-8273-6846-1
    1. Fashion merchandising—Study and teaching (Internship)
2. Clothing trade—Study and teaching (Internship)   I. Title
TT497.G73 1996
687' .023'42—dc20   94-48895
                                                CIP

*C*ontents

About the Author   xi
Acknowledgments   xiii
To the Academic Internship Sponsor   xv
To the Student   xix

CHAPTER 1

Getting Started   1

Internship How To's and Have To's   1
Recommended Time Line   3
Being an Effective Career Planner   4
Evaluating Your Job Seeking Assertiveness   6
Organizing Your Job Search   7
Networking   10

CHAPTER 2

Applying and Interviewing   13

Filling Out Job Application Forms   13
Writing Your Resume   23
    Creating an Effective Resume   23
    Guidelines for Resume Writing   24
    Using a Resume Organizational Worksheet   28
    Using Power Words in Your Resume   31
    Consulting Your Resume Checklist   33

Reviewing Your Resume 37
Purpose of the Resume 37
Key Components of the Resume 37
Do's and Don'ts 37
Constructing Your Letter of Application 38
The Structure of Letters of Application 39
Preparing Your Letter of Application 41
Approaching the Interview: The Cautious Employer and the
Internship Applicant 44
Interviewing Successfully 46
Before the Interview 46
During the Interview 47
Assessment Questions to Asked by Job Candidates 48
Assessment Questions to be Asked by Professional Interviewers 49
After the Interview 52
Writing a Follow-Up Letter 52
Writing a Follow-Up Letter After Your Employment Interview 53

CHAPTER 3

Getting Settled In

Getting Settled In 57
On-the-Job Tips 58
Present a Positive Attitude 58
Take Initiative 58
Project Assertiveness 59
Develop Professional Conduct and Work Habits 60
Five Rules for the Workplace 61
Ten Tips for Success 61
Changing Your Internship Plans 62
Your Internship Evaluation 63
Other Practical Considerations 63
Housing 63
Transportation 64
Budgeting 64
Dressing for Success 64

CHAPTER 4

Nature of the Organization

Nature of the Organization 67
Organization Classifications 67
Legal Forms of Organization 68

Types of Merchandise Sold   69
Extent of Nonstore Selling   70
Types of Services Offered   70
Extent of Departmentalization   71

CHAPTER 5

The Customer   91

Buying Motives   91
The Customer Decision Process   92
Demographics and Market Segmentation   93
    Lifestyles   94

CHAPTER 6

The Company Mission   97

The Mission Statement   97
Company Objectives and Goals   99
Market Positioning   100
The Competitive Environment   101

CHAPTER 7

The External Environment   107

The Economic Environment   108
The Social Environment   109
The Political/Legal Environment   110
The Natural Environment   110
The Technological Environment   111

CHAPTER 8

Product Identification   113

Product Levels   113
Product Classifications   114
Branding   118
Packaging and Labeling   119

CHAPTER 9

Customer Service

Customer Service 121

Types of Services 121
Levels of Service 123
Forms of Service 123
Customer Service Department 124
The Product Line 125
The Product Mix 125

CHAPTER 10

Pricing

Pricing 129

Factors in Pricing Decisions 130
Pricing Strategies 131

CHAPTER 11

Distribution

Distribution 143

Conventional Marketing Channels 143
Marketing Channel Flows 144
Vertical Marketing Channels 145
Horizontal and Multichannel Marketing Channels 146
Channel Design Alternatives 147
Channel Management 148
Physical Distribution 149

CHAPTER 12

Promotion

Promotion 151

Identifying the Target Market 151
Choosing a Message 152
Personal versus Nonpersonal Communication Channels 153
Choosing the Media Type 155
Setting the Promotion Budget 156
Setting the Promotion Mix 157
Visual Merchandising 161
Collecting Feedback 161

Appendix A	*Employer/Student/Academic Sponsor Agreement for the Internship*	163
Appendix B	*Weekly Activity Report Forms*	165
Appendix C	*Evaluation Forms*	181
Appendix D	*Career Options in the Fashion Industry*	191
Glossary		195
Index		207

About the author

Michele Granger is chairperson of the Fashion Program and coordinator of the Fashion Merchandising Program at Stephens College in Columbia, Missouri. At Stephens College, Ms. Granger presently serves on the Tenure and Promotion Committee and the Alumnae Recognition Committee. In addition, she has taught as an adjunct professor at Southwest Missouri State University in Springfield, Missouri. Her involvement in business and fashion outside of the college includes membership in the National Retail Federation, Women's Network, and The Fashion Group International. Recently, Ms. Granger was selected by the International Textiles and Apparel Association as a recipient of the Special Recognition for Outstanding Fashion Merchandising Education award.

Her professional background includes fourteen years of experience in fashion merchandising as a retail buyer for a thirteen-unit ladies' and children's apparel chain, a fashion coordinator, a manufacturers' representative, and a specialty store owner. Ms. Granger holds a dual Bachelor of Science degree in Clothing and Textiles and Business Administration from Central Missouri State University, Warrensburg, Missouri, and a Master of Science degree in Textiles and Apparel Management from the University of Missouri in Columbia, Missouri. She is currently a student in the doctoral program of Nova Southeastern University.

Acknowledgments

To my parents, Sally and John Granger, for giving me roots and wings. To my sister Patricia and my brother Joseph for their support and encouragement. To my beautiful daughter, Annie, to whom I hope to pass on the lessons I learned from my parents. Special gratitude to my colleagues at Stephens College: Donna Virden, Jeanne Powell, Laura Bliss, Mary Ruppert, and Sarah Riley, who are more friends than coworkers. Grateful acknowledgment to Carey Kaltenbach for providing the original material upon which the letter of application and follow-up letter content is based. Thanks to Debi Wooton for her typing assistance and to all of my students, past and present, for sharing a passion for fashion and for always teaching this teacher. Much appreciation to Jean Hamilton, my graduate advisor, for getting me started on this project. Finally, thank you to Mary McGarry of Delmar and the following reviewers for their insightful suggestions and support: Jennifer Friestad, Anoka/Ramsey Community College; Joan McCrillas, Johnson County Community College; Theresa Robinson, Middle Tennessee State University.

To the academic internship sponsor

An internship can be an extraordinary experience for a student. The purpose of this guide is to help the student gain as much from the experience as possible. While workbooks exist for the retailing internship, what does the student do who manages to secure a position with an apparel manufacturers representative, an accessory importer in a large city, a fashion forecasting service, or the costume collection of a museum?

This guide is intended for the student employed in any segment of the textile and apparel industry. It can be applied to any organization anywhere along the channel of distribution and serving any market segment(s). It is based on a marketing model focusing on an organization's control over product, promotion, pricing, and distribution decisions, all with the intent of better serving and capitalizing on the target market(s).

Certain assumptions have been made in the preparation of this guide. These are that:

1. The student user will have a background in marketing principles.
2. The guide will be used by an upper-level student who is conceptually mature.
3. The student will adjust questions to directly relate to her internship organization.
4. Responses to questions will be succinct and brief.
5. The internship employer and the student will review the guide prior to beginning the internship experience.

In each section of this guide, the student will find the topic introduced through a brief narrative. Examples are given as to how the topic might be applied to all organizations. The student must be sophisticated enough to read the introduction and the examples, look critically at his organization, and redefine the question in an appropriate way, if necessary. This means that the student must partially provide the question as well as the answer. The student familiar with the case study method will have an advantage. As she will be asked to evaluate, analyze, criticize, speculate, and make connections between concepts and practice, the student must be past the point in terms of intellectual maturity of depending on another to always generate the question that must be asked. The intent is to encourage critical thinking.

This guide is designed to help the student with the formation of questions that are pertinent to analyzing his internship organization from a marketing perspective. Conceptually, the guide asks the student to look critically at his place of work (retail store, museum, factory, design workroom, etc.) as an organization with its own unique way of relating to its:

- customers;
- environment to which it must respond;
- unique competitive surroundings;
- formal and informal power structure;
- individual resource and personnel limitations; and
- way of manipulating the variables of what it offers (product), how it informs potential customers (promotion), how it determines what to charge or how to pay (pricing), and how it will get that product to its customers (distribution).

In responding to the sections of this guide, the student is encouraged not to be merely descriptive. Once the description is formulated, she should take the perspective of a business consultant to this organization and ask, "In what new ways should this organization look at the issue?" If, for example, the issue of social responsibility is one that has apparently never been raised, the student should ask: (1) Why has it not been raised? (2) What are the social responsibility implications for this organization? (3) What specific issues of social responsibility might the internship organization respond to and how?

In addition, the student is required to examine not only his organization but to also think about organizations similar to his internship operation, about its competition, and about the topic as it affects similar organizations in general. The student cannot assume that all retailers, for example, buy only from manufacturers' representatives who visit them in their stores because that is how it is done in his internship retail outlet, nor can he assume that all apparel manufacturers do pattern drafting by computer just because his organization is fortunate enough to have state-of-the-art equipment.

A Guide to Analyzing Your Fashion Industry Internship has been designed to (1) ask for minimum written requirements from the internship employer; (2) allow for any time length required by the academic institution and/or the internship employer; and (3) respond to all types of internship experiences available in the fashion industry. Due to the tremendous diversity of occupations and businesses within the fashion industry, a limitation of this guide is its inability to ask specific questions as they relate to particular jobs and organizations. You are encouraged to "edit" the guide as you deem appropriate by deleting sections of the text that do not reflect the student's internship experience or by substituting assignments that more directly fit the student's internship organization. This permits you to "customize" the student's internship and provides for adjustments necessary to meet the requirements of the academic program.

The *Weekly Activity Report* forms in Appendix B can be used, for example, during a four-week intersession or a fourteen-week semester internship experience. Before starting the internship experience, the student is requested to establish a time frame for completing the chapters in the guide. She may submit the *Weekly Activity Report* forms to the academic internship sponsor following the end of the internship experience or each week, to be determined by the academic internship sponsor. The internship employer is requested to complete the *Student Evaluation* form in Appendix C at the conclusion of the internship experience.

Finally, it is critical to recognize that the successful internship experience requires a cooperative partnership between three parties: the academic internship sponsor, the internship employer, and the student. The *Employer/Student/Academic Sponsor Agreement* form (Appendix A) connects the three partners through a mutual commitment, prior to the student beginning the internship experience, to maintain channels of communication. Open communication and the common objective of seeing that the student succeeds are prerequisites for a positive experience. An internship can truly be a win/win situation for all partners. The student can benefit from hands-on experience through the opportunity to apply academic theory to the "real world" and, possibly, to procure the additional benefit of post-graduation employment. The internship employer can gain a new and enthusiastic perspective through the student's eyes, as well as a pool for future employees. The academic internship sponsor is exposed to various fashion industry businesses and provided with an excellent opportunity to assess not only student performance on the job but to evaluate the relationship between academic course content and current industry needs and trends.

To the student

Congratulations! You are about to set out on an exciting adventure in the fashion industry—the internship. For some of you, this may be your first work experience. Others may have been employed for years as a sales associate in a specialty store, cashier in a discount store, or receptionist for an apparel manufacturer. Regardless of your prior level of experience (or inexperience), the internship provides several new opportunities and challenges. You will:

- be exposed to the business organization as a whole;
- construct a written analysis of the internship organization through the completion of this guide and your *Weekly Activity Report* forms;
- fulfill an academic requirement through hands-on experience; and
- be evaluated by both your employer and academic internship sponsor.

These challenges will require that you develop a new perspective: that of a business consultant who analyzes the organization in its entirety. The purpose of this guide is to provide structure for your analysis of the organization as a whole, to help you gain as much from the internship experience as possible. This guide is intended for the student employed in any segment of the textile and apparel industry. It can be applied to any organization anywhere along the channel of distribution and serving any market segment(s). The guide is based on a marketing model, focusing on organization's control over product, promotion, pricing, and distribution decisions, all with the intent of better serving and capitalizing on the target market(s).

Certain assumptions have been made in the preparation of this guide. These are that:

1. You have a basic understanding of marketing principles.
2. You are an upper-level student who is conceptually mature.
3. You will adjust questions to directly relate to your internship organization.
4. Your responses to questions will be succinct and brief.
5. You will review the guide with the internship employer prior to beginning the internship experience.

In each section of this guide, you will find the topic introduced through a brief narrative. Examples are given as to how the topic might be applied to all organizations. You are requested to read the introduction and the examples, look critically at your organization, and redefine the question in an appropriate way, if necessary. You cannot always depend on the guide to generate the specific question that must be asked. You are asked to evaluate, analyze, criticize, speculate, and make connections between concepts and practice. If you are familiar with the case study method, you will have an advantage. This means that you must partially provide the question as well as the answer. The intent is to encourage critical thinking. The guide is designed to help you with the formation of the questions.

Conceptually, the guide asks you to look critically at your organization (retail store, museum, factory, design workroom, etc.) as an organization with its own unique way of relating to its:

- customers;
- environment to which it must respond;
- unique competitive surroundings;
- formal and informal power structure;
- individual resource and personnel limitations; and
- way of manipulating the variables of what it offers (product), how it informs potential customers (promotion), how it determines what to charge or how to pay (pricing), and how it will get that product to its customers (distribution).

In responding to the sections of this guide, you are asked to be not merely descriptive. Once the description is formulated, take the perspective of a business consultant to this organization and ask, "In what new ways should this organization look at the issue?" If, for example, the issue of social responsibility is one that has apparently never been raised, you should ask: (1) Why has it not been raised? (2) What are the social responsibility implications for this organization? (3) What specific issues of social responsibility might the internship organization respond to and how?

In addition, you are required to examine not only your organization but also to think about organizations similar your internship operation, about its competition, and about the topic as it affects similar organizations in general. You cannot assume that all retailers, for example, buy only from manufacturers' representatives who visit them in their stores because that is how it is done in your internship retail outlet, nor can you assume that all apparel manufacturers do pattern drafting by computer just because your organization is fortunate enough to have state-of-the-art equipment.

A Guide to Analyzing Your Fashion Industry Internship has been designed to (1) respond to all types of internship experiences available in the fashion industry, (2) allow for any time length required by the academic institution and/or the internship employer, and (3) ask for minimum written requirements from the internship employer.

The *Weekly Activity Report* forms in Appendix B can be used, for example, during a four-week intersession or a fourteen-week semester internship experience. Before starting the internship experience, you are requested to establish a time frame for completing the chapters in the guide. You may submit the *Weekly Activity Report* forms to the academic internship sponsor following the end of the internship experience or each week, to be determined by the academic internship sponsor. Your internship employer is requested to complete the *Student Evaluation* form in Appendix C at the conclusion of the internship.

Finally, the issue of confidentiality is one that should be understood before you begin your internship experience. Internship employers have varying degrees of comfort regarding the type and amount of information they provide to you. While one internship employer will completely open his books to a student, another will prefer total privacy when it comes to inventory shortages, payroll, sales volume, etc. If your internship employer is discreet regarding specific information you believe is necessary to complete the guide successfully, you will need to do some independent research to locate industry norms. The National Retail Federation annually publishes *Merchandising and Operating Reports*, a directory that contains industry averages (low, mid, and high) for most merchandising statistics (maintained markup, stock turn, shortages, sales per square feet, etc.) for all types of retail operations. Some internship employers may feel more comfortable with providing you with a range for such statistics, rather than specific data.

Regardless of the amount of information the internship employer will supply, you owe it to your employer to be responsible for any level of exposure you receive. A business consultant respects the employer's right to privacy. This means that, as a professional, it is inappropriate for you to discuss with others (including fellow employees) information you are exposed to such as hourly wages, sales performance, interpersonal relationships, etc., as they pertain to your internship organization. Discretion is the key. Good luck as you begin your internship!

Getting Started

INTERNSHIP HOW TO'S AND HAVE TO'S

When should I start to plan for my internship?
Begin to plan two semesters prior to when you expect to complete the internship. For example, start planning during a current fall semester for an internship during the following summer.

What do I do first?
Before contacting employers, it is important to clarify your goals and expectations of the internship experience. What do you want to do in the internship? Sell? Buy? Learn to plan and coordinate fashion shows? Work on finance, control, or visual merchandising? Learn the functions of personnel? Design? Construct patterns?

Now, I am ready to contact employers, right?
Not quite. The next step involves research: researching employers and employment opportunities.

So, what next?
Now you are faced with an important choice ... do you want to apply for an existing internship or should you create your own?

For example, Halls Merchandising Inc. (HMI) and Saks Fifth Avenue, both in Kansas City, offer existing internship programs. For HMI and Saks, the opportunity is available from November through January. Applying for these programs requires careful, long-range planning to anticipate a lighter academic load during the appointed internship semester. Unlike a "create-your-own" approach, an interview for an existing internship clearly resembles a real job interview.

If you are interested in returning home or perhaps working in your college town during the school year or summer, you may find it advisable to identify the specific employer you are interested in and to apply directly to that organization.

Once I have decided between creating my own internship or applying for an existing one, how do I present myself?
It is necessary to develop an appropriate resume and letter of application describing yourself, your experiences, and what you are applying for.

How many companies should I apply to for an internship?
Although there is no right answer—it depends entirely upon your own personal goals and objectives—you should consider submitting a minimum of five–ten applications.

Will I get paid for my internship?
Maybe. Some companies pay students the minimum hourly wage. Other organizations often do not pay for the internship experience. It is up to you to decide whether or not you will settle for an unpaid internship.

What if I receive more than one offer?
Lucky you! Choosing among offers is never easy. If, however, you have clarified your goals and objectives in applying for the internship early in your search, you will be in a better position to evaluate offers as they are made to you.

RECOMMENDED TIME LINE

The following schedule has been developed by internship students, alumni, and industry employers for students planning to intern during the summer session. If you prefer to complete your internship during a fall or spring semester or during a semester intersession, adjust the plan as needed.

September—Attend resume workshops and practice interviewing sessions, attend student internship presentations, and network with your peers about internship opportunities.

October—Research potential employers (*Fairchild's, Sheldon's, Store's, Standard & Poor, Women's Wear Daily,* graduate file, etc.); read *A Guide to Analyzing Your Fashion Industry Internship* thoroughly.

November—Write your resume and letters of application; continue researching for potential employers.

December—After your resume and letters of application have been proofread several times, have them printed.

January—Mail your letters of application and resume to prospective employers.

February—Follow up on inquiry letters, and schedule phone and/or personal interviews.

March—Interview during spring break, if needed; continue contacting potential employers.

April—Register for summer session internship.

May—Turn in internship application before leaving campus.

June, July, and/or August—Complete actual internship (on-the-job work hours).

BEING AN EFFECTIVE CAREER PLANNER

To be an effective career planner, use the following helpful hints:

1. Understand yourself and your current interests, values, aptitudes, and abilities.
2. Have a general understanding of the world of work. This requires exposing yourself to various work environments through paid or unpaid jobs, talking to people working in fashion industry career fields, and reading independently to investigate job and career options.
3. Identify your values in terms of career payoffs. In other words, know what is important to you—money, status, influence, the opportunity to make a difference, etc. How will your career affect your total lifestyle? Select an internship that provides the right environment for you.
4. Recognize that getting a job is a job in itself. Plan to spend time and effort toward your job search. It is an investment in your future.

Below you will find a schedule to assist you in organizing your job search.

JOB HUNTING WORK SCHEDULE

Week of _______________________________

Estimated Hours To Be Spent

Activity	M	T	W	Th	F	S	Sn
Self-Research							
Job Market Research							
Telephone Calls							
Letter Writing							
Job Interviews							
Other							
Daily Totals							

Weekly Total _________ hours

EVALUATING YOUR JOB SEEKING ASSERTIVENESS

How assertive are you (or will you be) as you interview for your internship position? Listed below are questions that will help you evaluate yourself:

Yes   No

_____   _____   Do you make an effort to research the company before the interview?

_____   _____   Do you prepare several questions that you want to ask?

_____   _____   If an interviewer asks a personal question unrelated to the job, can you tactfully call it to his attention?

_____   _____   If an interviewer gives you a hypothetical job-related problem, would you have enough confidence in your ability to respond in a timely and succinct manner?

_____   _____   If the interviewer seems distracted or uninterested during your interview, would you be able to steer the interview back on track and gain her attention?

_____   _____   When you meet the interviewer, would you be the first to introduce yourself and begin the conversation?

_____   _____   If the interviewer continually interrupts when you are responding to his questions or when giving information about yourself, can you politely handle this?

_____   _____   If the interviewer never gives you the opportunity to talk about yourself and you only have five minutes remaining in the interview, have you thought about phrases or ways to redirect the interview and regain control of the process?

_____   _____   When the interviewer is beginning to close the interview, do you ask questions concerning how you stand, what the determining factors are for candidate selection, and by what date you will have an answer?

ORGANIZING YOUR JOB SEARCH

Organization calls for a systematic way of recording and filing the information that you gather on prospective employers. Index cards are ideal for this purpose. As you gather pertinent information on job prospects, record it on the cards, one company or job prospect to a card. Enter the name, address, and phone number of the company on the face of the card, and add any other information that you feel would be useful, such as the nature of the company's products or services, names and titles of principal officers, the person you should contact, locations of branch offices, etc. The back of the card may be used to write notes on correspondence, phone calls, interviews, and needed follow-up work.

JOB SEARCH WORKSHEET

Job Target:

(Use a separate sheet for each job target.)

____

____

____

Telephone Calls or Letters:

Date	Person/ Organization	Phone #/ Address	Objective	Results

Specific Research Objectives:

Date	Sources to Contact	Objective	Results

Other Objectives:

(People with whom to network, information interviews, professional association meetings, etc.)

NETWORKING

Internship Resources: Where Do You Find Internship Positions? Internship positions can be found by using the following resources:

1. Library—*Standard & Poor, Women's Wear Daily, Daily News Record, Earnshaw's,* and *Wall Street Journal* are just a few of the resources that may be available in the library to provide information on fashion retailers, manufacturers, trend forecasting services, and resident buying offices, among others. Additional resources include *Sheldon's Retail Directory, Fairchild's Directory,* and *Stores* magazine. For internships that are not fashion retailing, there are directories of textile, apparel, and accessories manufacturers, such as *The Fashion Guide.* Fashion Group International and International Textile and Apparel Association (ITAA) membership books can be used as resources for all types of fashion internships.

2. Faculty—Your faculty members will often have industry contacts and/or suggestions about resources for the type of internship position you may be seeking. Be sure to ask for their ideas. You may want to provide your faculty members with a resume and a brief description of your internship "wish list." They may hear about the ideal position for you later in the semester.

3. Alumni—You will have many occasions to meet with alumni from your college. Find the right moment to introduce yourself and ask about internship opportunities. If you are unable to visit with alumni while they are on campus, send notes on a later date.

4. Friends and Family—Let your friends and family know that you are looking for an internship. Tell them about the type of internship you are seeking, the location you would prefer, the guidelines for the internship experience (e.g., number of hours to work), etc. Ask them for names, titles, and addresses of industry contacts and refer to the person who helped you in your letter of application.

5. Fellow Students—Talk to your peers, especially those who have completed internships, about how, what, when, and where they secured their internships. These students may be

able to refer you to their internship employers. Sometimes their parents may have connections with retail operations or design firms.

6. Career Services Department of Your School—Most schools have counseling centers and/or career planning and placement offices that provide information regarding potential employers, on-campus recruiting, and the job search.

7. Direct Contact with Preferred Employers—Magazine advertisements and garment hang tags often contain address information for a company's headquarters. Write to the company to request an internship opportunity.

8. Apparel Marts—You may elect to contact the apparel mart director (e.g., Kansas City, Atlanta, Dallas, St. Louis, etc.) to ask about positions with the mart director's office or with the manufacturers' representatives.

9. Organizations—Some organizations, such as Fashion Group International, solicit members to provide internship opportunities for college students interested in pursuing a career in the fashion industry. Contact this type of professional organization in your area for possible internship opportunities.

10. Guest Speakers at Your School—Drop them thank you notes for their presentations and think of contacting them again when seeking an internship.

Figure 1-1 offers suggestions on how to construct a networking letter to alumni, friends, and others.

Be sure to send a typed letter so that you present yourself in a professional manner.

Date

Alumnus's or friend's name
Address

Dear ________________: *(If the alumnus is a recent graduate, it would be acceptable to address him by his first name. However, if the alumnus or friend has been out of college for several years and is much older than you, address the letter Ms./Mrs./Mr. ________________.)*

Begin by introducing yourself as a student at ____________ (school) in your ________ year, studying in the area of ________________. Tell the person how you obtained their name (your parents, fellow student, graduate file, etc.) and why you are writing (advice and/or information about a permanent career position after graduation, assistance with relocating to her city, or help in securing an internship). Be as specific as possible, while allowing yourself options.

In the second paragraph, you can talk about what your internship goals are and briefly mention a few important things that she should know about your background (for example, courses taken and work experiences). It is also helpful to include your resume.

In the third paragraph, thank her for any assistance she can give you. Ask her if she would agree to meet with you when you are in her area or if you could discuss your internship search with her by phone. Students have also had success with alumni and acquaintances choosing to write them back. This might be another way for you to establish contact.

Sincerely,

Your name
Address
Phone number (with area code)

Figure 1-1 *Sample letter for networking*

Be sure to send the alumnus or friend a thank-you note in appreciation of her time after you have talked or after she has written you.

This letter format was designed to give you some guidelines. Use your own good judgment in writing a letter that you feel comfortable with.

Applying and Interviewing

Once you have developed your resume and letter of application, you are ready to begin the first active step toward obtaining your internship: applying and interviewing for your internship. You will be presenting yourself "in person," rather than through the written picture provided by your resume. It is time to think on your feet.

FILLING OUT JOB APPLICATION FORMS

Many employers ask for a completed job application form even if you provide a resume. The information requested is basically the same on all applications: personal data, education, past work experience, and references. Each application will ask for the information in varying detail. Because many applications cannot be taken home and filled out, it is a good idea to carry an information sheet with you so that names, dates, and addresses of your past employment situations and job references are handy. Accuracy and neatness are important. Forms that are scratched out or left blank or contain misspelled words and unreadable writing do not make positive impressions.

Be sure to read the directions on a job application form carefully. The directions tell you exactly how to fill in the application and can save you a lot of time and errors. Try to avoid abbreviations unless they are commonly known, like state abbreviations such as PA, CA, and NY. Any questions not applying to you should be marked "Not Applicable," "N/A," or marked by drawing a line through the blank space. For questions concerning salary, you can state your expected salary in hourly or monthly terms, as a salary range, or simply write "open" or "negotiable."

An example of an employment application form for a retail operation is shown in Figure 2-1. A second example, shown in Figure 2-2, illustrates an employment application form for an apparel manufacturing and design firm.

THE LIMITED

EMPLOYMENT APPLICATION

As an equal opportunity employer, The Limited, Inc does not discriminate in hiring or terms and conditions of employment because of an individual's race, creed, color, sex, age, handicap or national origin.

_____ / _____ / _____
Date of Application

Position Desired: _____________

Schedule Desired: [ ] Full time [ ] Temporary
or or
[ ] Part time [ ] Permanent

Salary Expected: $ __________ per __________

Date Available: _____ / _____ / _____

PERSONAL INFORMATION

Last Name	First Name	Middle Name	Are you a Citizen of the U.S.? [ ] Yes [ ] No
Present Street Address	City	State	Zip	How long have you lived there? Yrs. Mo.
Previous Street Address	City	State	Zip	How long did you live there? Yrs. Mo.
Home Phone Number	Social Security Number	Are you under 18 years of age? Yes ☐ No ☐	

EDUCATION

Type of School	Name and Location of School	Degree/Area of Study	Number of Years Attended	Graduated (Check One)
HIGH SCHOOL	Name ____________ City ____ State ____			Yes ☐ No ☐
JUNIOR COLLEGE	Name ____________ City ____ State ____			Yes ☐ No ☐
COLLEGE	Name ____________ City ____ State ____			Yes ☐ No ☐
GRADUATE SCHOOL	Name ____________ City ____ State ____			Yes ☐ No ☐
OTHER	Name ____________ City ____ State ____			Yes ☐ No ☐

ACADEMIC AND PROFESSIONAL ACTIVITIES AND ACHIEVEMENTS

Academic and Professional Activities and Achievements, Awards, Publications or Technical-Professional Societies. Indicate type or name. Exclude organizations which indicate race, creed, color, sex, age, handicap or national origin of its members.

Date Awarded

SPECIAL SKILLS

Typing Speed __________ wpm.

Shorthand or Speedwriting __________ wpm.

Other Equipment Operated:

Other Skills applicable to position applied for

MILITARY SERVICE

Branch of Service	Technical Specialization	Rank Attained	Date Entered	Date Discharged
			___ / ___ mo. yr.	___ / ___ mo. yr.

01101310-4 (Rev. 5/91)

Figure 2-1 *Employment application—retail operation*

EMPLOYMENT HISTORY

List employment starting with your most recent position. Account for any time during this period that you were unemployed by stating the nature of your activities. If you have less than four places of employment, include personal references to be contacted. May we contact your present employer? [ ] Yes [ ] No

DATES	NAME AND ADDRESS OF EMPLOYER	POSITION HELD AND SUPERVISOR	LIST MAJOR DUTIES	WAGES	REASON FOR LEAVING
From: / mo. yr. To: / mo. yr.	Name / Address / Phone	Your Job Title / Supervisor		Starting / Final	
From: / mo. yr. To: / mo. yr.	Name / Address / Phone	Your Job Title / Supervisor		Starting / Final	
From: / mo. yr. To: / mo. yr.	Name / Address / Phone	Your Job Title / Supervisor		Starting / Final	
From: / mo. yr. To: / mo. yr.	Name / Address / Phone	Your Job Title / Supervisor		Starting	

MISCELLANEOUS

Is there any additional information involving a change of your name or assumed name that will permit us to check your work record?

If yes, please explain.

Have you ever been employed by A division of The Limited, Inc. before? [ ] Yes [ ] No	When	Where	Position

List Names of Friends or Relatives now employed by The Limited:

List any hobbies or special interests you have:

Have you ever been convicted of a crime? [ ] Yes [ ] No   If yes, please explain:

What is the present status of your health? (explain)	Amount of time lost from work during last two years. Please explain:
Do you have any impairment that would prevent you from performing the activities involved in the job(s) for which you applied. Please explain:	If there are any jobs for which you do not wish to be considered or duties you cannot perform because of physical, mental or medical disabilities, please explain:

PERSON TO CONTACT IN CASE OF EMERGENCY

This information is to facilitate contact in the event of an emergency and is not used in the selection process

Full Name	Address	Phone	Relationship to you?
Place of Employment	Address	Phone	

PLEASE READ THIS STATEMENT CAREFULLY

I hereby affirm that the information given me on this application for employment is complete and accurate. I understand that any falsification will be immediate grounds for dismissal. I authorize a thorough investigation to be made in connection with this application concerning my character, general reputation, personal characteristics and mode of living, whichever may be applicable. I understand that this investigation may include personal interviews with third parties, such as family members, business associates, financial sources, friends, neighbors or others with whom I am acquainted. I further understand that I have the right to make a written request within a reasonable period of time for a complete and accurate disclosure of the nature and scope of the investigation.

It is understood that, as a prerequisite to consideration for employment, I agree to submit to such future examinations, physical or other, as may be required by the company. The company will pay the reasonable cost of any such examination which may be required.

If I am hired, I agree that my employment and compensation can be terminated with or without cause and without notice at any time at the option of The Limited or myself. I understand that no store manager or other representative of The Limited other than a Vice-President has authority to enter into any agreement for employment for any specified period of time, or to make any agreement contrary to the foregoing.

I have read and affirm as my own the above statements.

_______________________   _______________________
Signature   Date

APPLICANTS IN THE STATE OF MARYLAND ONLY

Under Maryland law an employer may not require or demand any applicant for employment or prospective employment or any employee to submit to or take a polygraph, lie detector or similar test or examination as a condition of employment or continued employment. Any employer who violates this provision is guilty of a misdemeanor and subject to a fine not to exceed $100.

_______________________   _______________________
Signature   Date

Figure 2-1(cont.)   *Employment application—retail operation*

JHCollectibles.
Application For Employment

We consider applicants for all positions without regard to race, color, religion, creed, gender, national origin, age, disability, handicap, marital or veteran status, sexual orientation, or any other legally protected status.

If you need assistance in completing this application for employment or require a reasonable accommodation to the testing process, please notify the Personnel Department.

Position(s) Applied For	Location	Date of Application

How Did You Learn About Us?

☐ Advertisement   ☐ Friend   ☐ Walk-In

☐ Employment Agency   ☐ Relative   ☐ Other ______________

Last Name	First Name	Middle Name

Address	Number	Street	City	State	Zip Code

Telephone Number(s)	Social Security Number

If you are under 18 years of age, can you provide required proof of your eligibility to work?   ☐ Yes   ☐ No

Have you ever filed an application with us before?   ☐ Yes   ☐ No

If Yes, give date ______________

Have you ever been employed with us before?   ☐ Yes   ☐ No

If Yes, give date ______________

Are you currently employed?   ☐ Yes   ☐ No

May we contact your present employer?   ☐ Yes   ☐ No

Are you prevented from lawfully becoming employed in this country because of Visa or Immigration Status?
Proof of citizenship or immigration status will be required upon employment.   ☐ Yes   ☐ No

On what date would you be available for work? ______________

Are you available to work: ☐ Full Time   ☐ Part Time   ☐ Shift Work   ☐ Temporary

Are you currently on "lay-off" status and subject to recall?   ☐ Yes   ☐ No

Can you travel if a job requires it?   ☐ Yes   ☐ No

Have you been convicted of any felony, misdemeanor or other offense, which a reasonable person would view as substantially relating to the requirements and circumstances of the job for which you are applying?   ☐ Yes   ☐ No
If Yes, please explain ______________

WE ARE AN EQUAL OPPORTUNITY EMPLOYER

Figure 2-2 *Employment application—apparel manufacturing and design firm*

Educational Background

	Name and Address of School	Course of Study	Years Completed	Diploma Degree
Elementary School				
High School				
Undergraduate College				
Graduate Professional				
Other (Specify)				

Indicate any foreign languages you can speak, read and / or write			
	ABOVE AVERAGE	AVERAGE	BELOW AVERAGE
SPEAK			
READ			
WRITE			

Describe any specialized training, apprenticeship, skills, licences (ie. boiler, truck driver etc.) and extra-curricular activities.

Describe any specialized job-related training received in the United States Military. Be specific as to equipment used (ie. trucks, mechanical equipment, etc.)

Figure 2-2(cont.) *Employment application—apparel manufacturing and design firm*

Employment Experience

Start with your present or last job. Include any job-related military service assignments and volunteer activities. You may exclude organizations which indicate race, color, religion, gender, national origin, handicap or other protected status.

1.

Employer	Dates Employed		Work Performed
	From	To	
Address			
Telephone Number(s)	Hourly Rate/Salary		
	Starting	Final	
Job Title / Supervisor			
Reason for Leaving			

2.

Employer	Dates Employed		Work Performed
	From	To	
Address			
Telephone Number(s)	Hourly Rate/Salary		
	Starting	Final	
Job Title / Supervisor			
Reason for Leaving			

3.

Employer	Dates Employed		Work Performed
	From	To	
Address			
Telephone Number(s)	Hourly Rate/Salary		
	Starting	Final	
Job Title / Supervisor			
Reason for Leaving			

4.

Employer	Dates Employed		Work Performed
	From	To	
Address			
Telephone Number(s)	Hourly Rate/Salary		
	Starting	Final	
Job Title / Supervisor			
Reason for Leaving			

If you need additional space, please continue on a separate sheet of paper.

List professional, trade, business or civic activities and offices held.
You may exclude membership which would reveal gender, race, religion, national origin, age, ancestry, disability or other protected status:

Figure 2-2(cont.) *Employment application—apparel manufacturing and design firm*

Additional Information

Other Qualifications

Summarize special job-related skills and qualifications acquired from employment or other experience.

____

____

____

Specialized Skills   Check Skills/Equipment Operated

		Production/Mobile Machinery (list):	Other (list):
__CRT/Terminal	__Fax		
__PC	__Lotus 1-2-3	____________	____________
__Calculator	__Phone System	____________	____________
__Typewriter	__Wordperfect	____________	____________
__Cash Register		____________	____________

State any additional information you feel may be helpful to us in considering your application.

____

____

____

References

1. ____ (   ) __________
   (Name)   Phone #

   ____
   (Address)

2. ____ (   ) __________
   (Name)   Phone #

   ____
   (Address)

3. ____ (   ) __________
   (Name)   Phone #

   ____
   (Address)

Figure 2-2(cont.)   *Employment application—apparel manufacturing and design firm*

NAME:

FOR PERSONNEL DEPARTMENT USE ONLY

Position(s) Applied For Is Open:　　☐ Yes　　　☐ No

Position(s) Considered For: ______________________________

____

Date ________________

NOTES:

POSITION:

DATE:

Figure 2-2(cont.)　*Employment application—apparel manufacturing and design firm*

Applicant's Statement

I certify that answers given herein are true and complete to the best of my knowledge.

I authorize investigation of all statements contained in this application for employment as may be necessary in arriving at an employment decision.

This application for employment shall be considered active for a period of time not to exceed 45 days. Any applicant wishing to be reconsidered for employment beyond this time period should inquire as to whether or not applications are being accepted at that time.

I hereby understand and acknowledge that, unless otherwise defined by applicable law, any employment relationship with this organization is of an *"at will"* nature, which means that the Employee may resign at any time and the Employer may discharge Employee at any time. It is further understood that this *"at will"* employment relationship may not be changed by any written document or by conduct unless such change is specifically acknowledged in writing by an authorized executive of this organization.

In the event of employment, I understand that false or misleading information given in my application or interview(s) may result in discharge. I understand, also, that I am required to abide by all rules and regulations of the employer.

I affirm that everything is true and correct, and I acknowledge that I can be terminated at anytime if it turns out that any information I supply is false. I affirm that I have a genuine intent and no other purpose in applying for a job with the company.

I further understand that my employment may be conditioned on satisfactory results of a physical examination, including substance abuse screening. Refusal to participate following receipt of a conditional offer will result in the rejection of my application.

____   _______________
Signature of Applicant   Date

FOR PERSONNEL DEPARTMENT USE ONLY

Arrange Interview ☐ Yes   ☐ No

Remarks ____

____
INTERVIEWER   DATE

Employed ☐ Yes ☐ No   Date of Employment _______________

Job Title _______________   Hourly Rate/
                              Salary _______ Department_______________

By _______________________________________
NAME AND TITLE   DATE

FORM NO. 410-008

Figure 2-2(cont.) *Employment application—apparel manufacturing and design firm*

WRITING YOUR RESUME

Creating an Effective Resume

What is a resume?

A **resume** is a one- or two-page summary of your education, experience, and skills. As the resume is a primary tool in a job search, it may require hours of work and several drafts to create the most effective resume. Because employers who receive your resume with its accompanying letter of application will assess both its form and content, every effort must be made to ensure an effectively written and well-presented resume.

What is the focus of a resume?

A resume is not a biographical summary of your life but a statement that highlights your qualifications for employment in a particular position or career field. In preparing a resume for one type of internship experience, certain information may be left out that would be included in a resume for another type of internship. Your resume should focus attention on your qualifications and achievements and on contributions you can make to an employer. Keep it up-to-date. Rewrite and reprint it often.

What are some general guidelines for resume writing?

- **Style**—Resumes are written in an abbreviated style with incomplete sentences. "I" is understood.
- **Design**—Plan your layout to lead the reader to important entries. Use short entries (no more than four or five lines in a block). Your resume should be one or two pages long, depending on your background.
- **Mechanics**—Use a good quality bond paper and have your resume printed clearly.

Guidelines for Resume Writing

Specific guidelines for resume writing are:

Typical Headings

What To Put In—What To Leave Out

Personal Data
- ❏ Always include your name, address, and phone number (permanent and local to make yourself optimally accessible).
- ❏ Evaluate your personal characteristics for their job significance. A prospective employer is usually interested in your qualifications, not your appearance.
- ❏ A photograph is unnecessary and it is illegal for an employer to request one.
- ❏ Do not include data on gender, age, race, marital status, number of dependents, height, or weight. If you have questions on whether or not to include data, ask yourself if it is relevant to performance on the job; if not, omit it.

Job Objective
Make a concise, positive statement about the type of work you are seeking, including immediate internship and long-range career goals. Indicate the position or positions you think yourself best qualified for, keeping the objective broad enough to fit several job possibilities (if that suits your needs) and specific enough to enable tailoring to individual employers. If you are aiming at a diverse group of jobs, leave the objective off the resume and include it in your more specific letter of application.

Education
List your highest level of formal education first; then the institution, major and minor (if applicable), and degree earned followed by the reverse chronological listing of other levels of education.

GPA and special courses related to job objective may be included. If they relate to your objective and would be impressive, include them; if not, do not.

Do not include high school if you have college education or post-high school training.

Work History   When describing work experience, do not simply say, "I was great," but explain *why* you were. Generally, cite only experience that is related to the job you are seeking. Some employers want to know all previous experience, thinking part-time work during college shows initiative. Other employers are only interested in experience related to the job. Decide for yourself which approach is stronger for you. List your most recent job first.

Describe for each job:

Job duties—tasks performed, emphasizing those requiring the highest degree of skill and judgment. Indicate your specialization and any duties beyond your regular assignment.

Scope of responsibility—did you hold a supervisory position? How many people did you supervise? Describe your position.

Accomplishments—outline the outstanding results achieved by your efforts. If possible, give concrete facts and figures, rather than generalities.

Work actions—utilize words such as "developed," "organized," "planned," "researched," etc., that denote action and/or responsibility in describing work performed.

Volunteer work, field experiences, and practicum opportunities—should be included in your work history, especially if they are related to your professional objective.

Related Professional Information

This category should include:

- ❑ Licenses and certificates currently held
- ❑ Honors, scholarships, awards, fellowships earned
- ❑ Professional organization memberships and offices held
- ❑ Publications
- ❑ Affiliations with civic and community groups, including volunteer work
- ❑ Special skills such as fluency in a foreign language, typing, operation of business machines, computer skills, etc.
- ❑ Hobbies and outside interests
- ❑ Internship or externship experiences
- ❑ Extracurricular activities

References

References can be handled a couple of different ways. Currently, the most preferred method seems to be to list your references' names, addresses, and phone numbers on a separate sheet or in your letter of application. Many employers value getting a telephone recommendation over a more general written letter.

Another method is to state on your resume, "References Available Upon Request." Make sure each of your references has agreed in advance to take time to write letters or take phone calls concerning your experiences and skills.

Work supervisors, academic advisors, professors, etc., make some of the best references. It is important to have references who have something positive and specific to say about your work performance. This is the type of information the potential employer wants to know.

If you list your references on your resume, follow this model:

References

Name ____

Title ____

Address ____

____

____

Phone (work) ____________________________________

Phone (home) ____________________________________

(List home and work telephone numbers only if your reference approves. Remember to include area codes.)

USING A RESUME ORGANIZATIONAL WORKSHEET

Directions: Use this worksheet to help you collect and organize information you may want to use on your resume. **DO NOT use this as the format for your final resume**—only use it as a worksheet. Include all details needed such as dates of employment, employers' titles, addresses, zip codes, area codes, etc. Additional sheets of paper for extra space to organize your experience, education, and activities sections may be needed.

Personal Data (information):

Name ____

Current Address:
Street ____

City _________________________ State _______________ Zip _____________________

Home phone (area code) _______________ Work phone (area code) ___________________

Permanent Address:
Street ____

City _________________________ State _______________ Zip _____________________

Home phone (area code) _______________ Work phone (area code) ___________________

Internship Objectives (type of position or job):

____

____

____

____

____

Education:

____

____

Course Highlights or Related Courses:

____

____

____

Experience (include full-time, part-time, summer, practicum, and internships):

____

____

____

____

____

Competencies and Skills—Optional (computer/software knowledge; language fluency; technical skills):

____

____

____

Activities and Honors:

____

____

Related Professional Information (certification, publications, professional/honorary organizational memberships, offices held, volunteer work):

____

____

____

____

____

____

Using Power Words in Your Resume

Your use of the following words will give your resume the look of achievement:

Accomplished	Coached	Drafted
Achieved	Commended	Dramatized
Acquired	Compiled	Doubled
Adapted	Completed	
Administered	Conceived	Earned**
Advanced to*	Condensed	Edited
Aided	Conducted	Effected
Allocated	Consolidated	Eliminated
Amplified	Constructed	Employed
Analyzed	Consulted	Enforced
Answered	Contributed	Enhanced
Anticipated	Contrived	Established
Appointed	Controlled	Evaluated
Appraised	Converted	Examined
Approval	Correlated	Executed
Arbitrated	Counseled	Exhibited
Arranged	Created	Expanded
Assembled	Crisis-solving	Expedited
Assisted		Experienced
Assumed	Delegated	Extended
Attained	Delivered	
Augmented	Demonstrated	Fabricated
Authored	Designed	Facilitated
Awarded	Detailed	Focused
	Determined	Formed
Bargained	Developed	Formulated
Began	Devised	Fortified
Broadened	Devoted	Fostered
Built	Directed	Founded
	Discovered	
Calculated	Dispensed	Generated
Catalogued	Displayed	Governed
Chaired	Distributed	Graduated
Clarified		Guided

Handled
Harmonized
Headed

Imagined
Implemented
Inspired
Installed
Instituted
Instructed
Insured
Integrated
Interpreted
Interviewed
Introduced
Invented
Investigated

Justified

Lectured
Led
Licensed
Listed

Maintained
Managed
Mastered
Medicated
Meditated
Moderated
Modified
Monitored
Motivated

Negotiated
Nominated

Observed
Operated
Ordered
Organized
Oriented
Originated
Overcame
Overhauled

Participated
Performed
Persuaded
Pioneered
Planned
Predicted
Prepared
Presented
Preserved
Presided
Processed
Produced
Programmed
Promoted
Proposed
Provided

Received
Recommended
Reconciled
Recorded
Recruited
Rectified
Reduced
Reestablished
Rehearsed
Reinforced
Remodeled
Reorganized

Reported
Represented
Researched
Responsible for
Reshaped
Restored
Revamped
Reviewed
Revised

Scheduled
Selected
Served
Set up
Simplified
Sketched
Sold
Solved
Specialized
Spoke
Streamline
Substituted
Succeeded
Suggested
Supervised
Supervisor
Supported

Tasted
Taught
Tested and revised
Timed
Trained
Transferred
Trouble-shooting
Tutored

Unified
Unison

Updated	Verified	Widened
Upgraded	Volunteered	Won
Used		Worked
Utilized		Wrote

* "Advanced to" rather than "promoted to"

** "Earned" rather than "was given" indicates a person who does things rather than receives them.

Hints:

- **Select** the best words for your resume.
- **Use** parallel phrase construction.
- **Always** use the same tense/ending on words.
- **Avoid** using the same verb more than once.
- **Allow** the format to emerge from your information rather than fitting your data into someone else's format.

Consulting Your Resume Checklist

Before completing work on your resume, make sure that each of the following areas have been appropriately prepared:

Personal Data

- ❑ Is everything current?
- ❑ Have you made yourself fully accessible (local and home address; phone numbers with area codes)?
- ❑ Are your characteristics significant for the job?

Job Objective

- ❑ Are your short-term and long-term goals included?
- ❑ Have you kept all possibilities open for all various positions?
- ❑ Have you kept qualifications specific, yet not too confining?
- ❑ Should your qualifications be included in cover letter instead/as well?

Education

- ❑ Does the order of your education start with the most recent?
- ❑ Have you included too much experience that is not directly related to your internship interests?
- ❑ Should you list course highlights?

Work History

- ❑ Is your experience related to the job you are seeking?
- ❑ Have you listed your most recent job first?

An example of a completed resume for internship, Figure 2-3, follows.

PATRICIA McCOY

Campus Address	**Permanent Address**
Tower Hall, Box 3922	300 West 14th Avenue
Stephens College	Apartment 1-C
Columbia, Missouri 65215	St. Louis, Missouri 63021
(314) 555-7402	(314) 555-4213

Objective: To obtain a retailing internship in the fashion industry that will allow me to use and expand upon my present skills while preparing me for future career employment.

Education: Bachelor of Science in Fashion Merchandising, an interdepartmental degree in Business Administration and Fashion, Stephens College, Columbia, Missouri. Anticipated graduation date: May 199X.
Related Business Administration Courses

Essentials of Business	Retailing
Management	Accounting I and II
Marketing	Finance

Work Experience: *Supervisor,* Bressler's Thirty-Three Flavors, St. Louis, MO, Summer 199X.
Served as night manager of store and supervised team of five coworkers. Handled responsibilities for daily closing of business.

Sales Associate, Express, St. Louis, MO, Summers 199X, 199X.
Assisted customers, checked in merchandise, and stocked floor. Created interior displays; cashiered.

Desk Hostess, Stephens College, Columbia, MO, 199X-9X.
Responsible for opening and closing residence hall; assisted visitors and students; handled telephone calls and messages.

Figure 2-3 *Sample resume for internship*

Honors/Activities: Pi Phi Rho, Fashion Honorary Organization, 199X-9X
Vice President, Tower Hall, 199X-9X

References: Professor Laura Bliss, Fashion Merchandising Instructor
Stephens College
Columbia, Missouri 65215
(314) 555-7206

Professor Jeanne Powell, Academic Adviser
Stephens College
Columbia, Missouri 65215
(314) 555-7233

Ms. Mary Ruppert, Store Manager
Express
2009 Galleria
St. Louis, Missouri 64738
(314) 555-1025

Figure 2-3(cont.) *Sample resume for internship*

REVIEWING YOUR RESUME

After you have constructed a draft of your resume, it is important to take the time to review it carefully before it is printed and mailed. Below you will find information to help you critique your resume objectively.

Purpose of the Resume

The purpose of the resume is to provide a prospective employer with a concise overview of the highlights of your education and past work experience, as well as information about how to communicate with your references.

Key Components of the Resume

1. Name
2. Current and permanent addresses and phone numbers
3. Internship goal (optional)
4. Education (most recent to least recent)
5. Experience (most recent to least recent; may separate into subheadings)
6. Honors/Awards (optional)
7. Special interests (optional)
8. References
   a. Write out names and titles *or*
   b. Available on request

Do's and Don't's

Do:

1. Make the most of your experiences; this is essentially a sales document.
2. Use terminology that stresses managerial and leadership abilities.
3. Make sure document is flawless and professional looking.
4. Update your resume often.

5. Use same paper stock for your resume, letter of application, and envelope.
6. Follow up mailing with a phone call to the company if you do not hear from them in a reasonable length of time.
7. Center your resume on the page.
8. Try to keep your resume to one page.

Don't:

1. Exaggerate your experiences.
2. Understate your experiences.
3. Settle for a resume with spelling or grammatical errors!
4. Send a resume with additional handwritten information on the side or on an additional page.
5. Hand-write a resume.
6. Badger companies in an unprofessional manner.
7. Run all resume components together, making it difficult to read.
8. Make your resume needlessly long.

CONSTRUCTING YOUR LETTER OF APPLICATION

You're not finished yet! A letter of application should accompany your resume.

In writing to apply for a job or to request a job interview, you should include your resume **and** a letter of application. In a nutshell, a **letter of application** is a brief explanation about what job you are interested in and how you heard about it. Its intent is to summarize your qualifications for the job. The letter of application includes only the relevant facts, mentioning that additional information is contained in the accompanying resume. It provides an opportunity to specify any special reason you have for applying with the company, such as a specific internship goal. In the conclusion of the letter of application, you may mention that you are available for an interview at the convenience of the addressee, or may indicate when you will be available (for instance, when your job or classes leave you free.)

On the next few pages, you will find information about the how-to's of constructing a letter of application. In addition, you will find a sample letter of application for use in preparing a letter of your own.

A letter of application creates a first impression of you. It ought, then, to observe the conventions governing such communication. No employer wants to hire an applicant to whom he will have to teach such points. He cannot afford the time or the trouble. Thus, your expertise in letter writing is itself a job skill. Put another way, the form of a letter of application tells much more about you than the content on the page. And you cannot, of course, afford to present yourself badly, personally or professionally. Through letters, you will compete with others, sell yourself and your ideas, represent others, and seek favors (information, etc.). Obviously, no professional can be indifferent to the skills involved in this kind of communication.

The Structure of Letters of Application

Letters of application have three parts or sections. They are:

Opening

1. Explain who you are and what you want.
   a. Name-dropping: name + position + institution
   b. Summary beginning: graduation + date + degree
      + institution
2. State specifically the job or internship position for which you are applying.

Body

1. Explain why you are interested in this job.
2. Explain why you are interested in this employing unit.

There really is little reason for an employing unit to be interested in you if you are not interested in that employer. If you have not shown enough incentive to find out something about a prospective employer and her reputation, one is left wondering in what other areas you will fail to show motivation. You need not expend a lot of prose indicating why you are interested in an employer and her interests and in working for the employing unit. A good writer can express such genuine interest in a sentence or two—three at the most.

3. Indicate the date you will be available for employment.
4. Indicate your selling points.

A college education merely earns you the right to join other college graduates in applying for the same position. It neither distinguishes you from others nor earns any special considerations. What you must do is to point out any special skills, activities, experiences, courses, and people under whom you have studied that set you apart from the crowd. Saying that you are qualified means absolutely nothing! This section of a letter of application will earn you as much attention as you expend energy and thought in its writing.

Remember that an employer expects you to be an investment—to return to him more than eight hours of labor each day. As a professional, he expects intangible dividends from you—cooperation, genuine interest in the well-being of the enterprise, contributions of ideas, problem-solving, good judgment, continuous competency in your specialty, and potential skills that can some day serve you in managerial positions. Whatever you can do in a letter of application to *show* competency, professionalism, and potential, you must do. You must also rely, of course, on taste, reason, and a political frame of mind as guides in selling yourself to an employer.

Closing

1. Indicate that you are enclosing a data sheet listing references (the latter always by permission!).
2. Express a willingness to supply more data (credentials, for example) if asked do so.
3. Request an interview—at your correspondent's convenience (you may tactfully suggest a time when you are most available).
4. Quietly thank your correspondent for her consideration of you.

Preparing Your Letter of Application

Observe the following guidelines in preparing letters of application:

Writing business letters Whether you are requesting information about a company or applying for a job, your letters to businesses will be written to busy people who want to see quickly why you are writing and what they can do for you. Be straightforward, clear, objective, and courteous. Observe conventions of grammar and usage, since these not only make your writing clear but also impress a reader with your care and intelligence.

Using a standard form Business correspondence customarily adheres to one of several acceptable forms. Use either unlined white paper measuring at least 8½″ by 11″ or what is called letterhead stationery with your address printed on top of the sheet. Type the letter, single spaced, on only one side of the sheet. Follow a standard format for each of the letter's parts (Figure 2-4).

The return address heading of the letter gives your address (but *not* your name) and the date. (If you are using letterhead stationery, only the date must be added.) Align the lines of the heading on the left, and place the whole heading to the right of the page, allowing enough space above it so that the entire letter will be centered vertically on the page.

The inside address should show the name, title, and complete address of the person to whom you are writing, just as this information will appear on the envelope. Begin the address two lines below the heading at the left side of the page.

The salutation greets the addressee. Place it two lines below the address and two lines above the body of the letter. Always follow it with a colon, not a comma or dash. If you are *not* addressing a particular person, use a general salutation such as "Dear Sir" or "Dear Madam" or "Dear Courtney Classics" (the company name). Use Ms. as the title for a woman when she has no other title, when you do not know how she prefers to be addressed, or when you know that she prefers to be addressed as Ms. If you know a woman prefers to be addressed as Mrs. or Miss, use the appropriate title.

If you do not know the name of the human resource director (or the person to whom your letter is directed), you may want to take a moment to telephone the company and ask the receptionist for the person's name (and its correct spelling), title, and exact address. It takes a couple of minutes and a couple of dollars for a long distance call to get this information, yet it will move you miles forward in the interview process.

The body of the letter containing its contents begins at the left margin. Rather than indenting paragraphs, place an extra line of space between them so they are readily visible.

The letter's close, beginning two lines below the last line of the body, aligns at the left with the heading at the top of the page. Typical closes include "Yours truly" and "Sincerely." Only the first letter is capitalized, and the close is followed by a comma.

The signature of a business letter has two parts—a typed one, four lines below the close, and a handwritten one filling in the space. The signature should consist only of your name, written as you sign your checks and school documents.

Below the signature, at the left margin, you may want to include additional information such as:

- Enc. (something is enclosed with the letter)
- Copy to Joe Granger (a copy is being sent to the person named)
- EAR/sbr (the initials of the author/the initials of the typist)

The envelope of the letter should show your name and address in the upper left corner and the addressee's name, title, and address to the right of the center. Use an envelope that is the same width as your stationery and about a third the height. Fold the letter horizontally, in thirds.

A sample of a letter of application follows (Figure 2-4).

300 West 14th Avenue
Apartment 1-C
St. Louis, Missouri 63021
February 26, 199X

Ms. Annie Wilson
Human Resource Director
J.C. Penney, Inc.
200 East Stemmons Freeway
Dallas, Texas 24031

Dear Ms. Wilson:

In response to your announcement posted in the Fashion Office of Stephens College, I am applying for the summer job of intern to the merchandising staff of J.C. Penney ladies' wear division.

I am currently enrolled at Stephens College as a sophomore, with a major in Fashion Merchandising, an interdepartmental degree in Fashion and Business Administration. As the enclosed resume shows, I have worked at Express as a sales associate for nearly two years. In addition, I have gained hands-on experience in fashion show production and visual merchandising through my college coursework. My long-range goal is a career in retail buying. I believe my educational background and my work experience qualify me for your internship opening.

I am available for an interview during our spring break, March 15th through 23rd, as I will be in Dallas during this time period. My telephone number on campus is (314) 555-7402; at home, it is (314) 555-4213. I will contact you within the next two weeks to schedule an interview at your earliest convenience. Thank you, in advance, for your consideration.

Sincerely,

Patricia McCoy

Patricia McCoy

Enc.

Figure 2-4 *Sample letter of application*

APPROACHING THE INTERVIEW: THE CAUTIOUS EMPLOYER AND THE INTERNSHIP APPLICANT

There are two types of internship programs: formal and informal. The **formal internship program** is usually offered by a large company. In the formal program, a group of student interns go through a series of preplanned classes and activities. In contrast, the **informal internship program** is designed by the individual student and the employer. Together they develop a program that will meet the employer's needs, the student's objectives, and the requirements of the academic institution. Below you will find observations on both formal and informal internship programs.

As a former internship employer in the industry who is now an internship coordinator in academia, I have included some observations that may be helpful to you as you approach the interview process. For over a decade, I worked as a buyer, store owner, and manufacturers' representative in the fashion industry. In each of these career positions, I supervised student interns. From these personal experiences and through conversations with a wide variety of other intern employers, I believe the following observations are consistent and worth noting.

1. **Formal internship programs in retailing/fashion merchandising are often offered only during the academic semesters rather than during summer session.** Saks Fifth Avenue, Dillard's, Macy's, and Hall's are a few of the retail operations that offer structured internship programs with a limited number of openings. These are tough positions to secure and may require a semester away from school. Instead, you may decide to solicit an informal internship position.

2. **The term "internship" often frightens the employer with no formal internship program.** Always be honest with your prospective employer. However, you may want to negotiate your position before labeling it as an internship. For example, you may ask the employer if you'll work a minimum of 140 hours; if you'll receive a variety of exposures to all or most aspects of the business; and if your direct supervisor would be willing to complete an evaluation form on your work performance at the conclusion of your employment. You may want to clarify

that you would expect to primarily work as a sales associate or receptionist or design assistant (or whatever position for which you are applying) but would like the opportunity to view other departments. You may even offer to observe the other departments on your own personal time when not "on the clock." If all of this is agreeable to the prospective employer, then you could say something like, "This position just as we've discussed would fulfill the internship requirement in my degree program. Would that be acceptable to you?" Now is the ideal time to show the employer *A Guide to Analyzing Your Fashion Industry Internship* and to let him know that you are responsible for completing this guide on your own time.

In summary:

- You may want to ask for a *job* rather than an *internship* in order to obtain the opportunity to describe your needs.
- Let the employer know that *A Guide to Analyzing Your Fashion Industry Internship* structures the program for the employer and places the responsibility on the student. You do not need to find a formal internship program to fulfill your academic requirement.
- The student does 95% of the internship written work; the employer is only required to fill out an evaluation form. This is not always the case.

3. **Let the prospective employer know what you are bringing to the internship organization:** enthusiasm, education, work experience, etc. Let her know that you are willing to start at the bottom, "to go-fer": vacuum the showroom, run errands, stock the floors, answer the phone, etc. There is something to learn from every task, and an eager, flexible employee moves up the career ladder quickly.

Good luck with your internship search! Keep looking until you find the right position for you.

INTERVIEWING SUCCESSFULLY

Preparing for an interview is often just as important as the interview itself. Here are some guidelines for interviewing successfully.

Before the Interview

1. Practice
   a. Questions you may be asked
   b. Questions you want to ask about the position and organization
   c. Role-playing an interview
2. Self-assessment
   a. Goals
   b. Skills, abilities, accomplishments
   c. Work values (important factors you look for in a job)
   d. Experiences
   e. Personality
3. Research
   a. Obtain company literature
   b. Write or visit the organization
   c. Talk to people familiar with the organization
4. Obtain references
5. Plan ahead
   a. Attire to be worn to the interview
   b. Directions to the interview site
   c. Time of arrival (get there with at least 5-10 minutes to spare)

Summary of Pre-interview Considerations Keep the following in mind in preparing for your interview:

- Find out the exact place and time of the interview.
- Be certain you know the interviewer's name and how to pronounce it if it is looks difficult.
- Do some research on the company with which you are interviewing—talk to people and read the company literature to know what its products or services are, where its offices are located, what its growth has been, and how its prospects look for the future.

- Think of two or three good questions you would like to ask during your interview.
- Plan to arrive at the designated place for your interview a little early so that you will not feel rushed and worried about being on time.
- Plan to dress in a manner appropriate to the job for which you are interviewing.

During the Interview

1. Think positive.
   a. Be enthusiastic, interested, knowledgeable, and confident.
2. Relate to the interviewer.
   a. Build positive rapport with the interviewer.
   b. Listen and observe; relate yourself to the employer or position.
3. Watch your body language.
   a. Be aware of nervousness (fidgeting, shaking leg, tapping, etc.).
   b. Project confidence (eye contact, firm handshake, upright posture).
4. Be aware of the questions the employer asks.
   a. Answer with information relevant to the position.
   b. Provide a direct answer; avoid being long-winded.
5. Think about the questions you ask.
   a. They should indicate that you know something about the job.
   b. Avoid questions that could easily be answered elsewhere (through research).
   c. Obtain information you need to know to be satisfied with the job (interviewing is a two-way process).
   d. Salary and benefit questions should be asked after the job is offered.
6. Achieve effective closure.
   a. Ask when the employer expects to make a decision.
   b. Restate your interest and ability to perform the job.
   c. Show confidence and enthusiasm (smile, end with a firm handshake).

d. Obtain employer's business card, if possible (it may be useful when writing a thank-you letter).

Interview Questions Too many employment applicants spend all their time preparing for questions to be asked of them by employers. Too often, they fail to ask vital questions that would help them learn if a job is right for them. Although some applicants do have the opportunity for a second contact through a follow-up interview, others do not have this option. After the job offer has been received and accepted, it may be too late to ask significant questions.

Failing to ask important questions during the interview often leads to jobs that offer neither interest nor challenge. Too often, uninformed applicants accept positions hoping that these will develop into something more meaningful and rewarding later.

A guide for interview conversation is to prepare nine positive thoughts before you go for an interview:

- three reasons why you selected the employer to interview
- three reasons you particularly like the employer
- three assets you have that should interest the employer

Below you will find two lists of questions. The first list includes questions you may choose to ask the potential employer during the interview. The second list illustrates the types of questions that the prospective employer may ask you during the interview.

Assessment Questions to be Asked by Job Candidates

1. Where is the organization going? What plans or projects are being developed to maintain or increase its market share? Have many new product lines been decided upon recently? Is the sales growth in the new product line sustainable?
2. Who are the people with whom I will be working? May I speak with some of them?
3. May I have a copy of the job description? What might be a typical first assignment?
4. Do you have a performance appraisal system? How is it structured? How frequently will I be evaluated?

5. What is the potential for promotion in the organization? In promotions, are employees ever transferred between functional fields? What is the average time to get to _________ level in the career path? Is your policy to promote from within or are many senior jobs filled by experienced people from outside? Do you have a job posting system?

6. What type of training will I receive? When does the training program begin? Is it possible to move through your program faster? About how many individuals go through your internship program?

7. What is the normal routine of a _________ like? Can I progress at my own pace or is it structured? Do employees normally work overtime?

8. How much travel is normally expected? Is a car provided to traveling personnel?

9. How much freedom is given and discipline required of new people? How much input does the new person have? How much decision-making authority is given to new personnel?

10. How frequently do you relocate employees? Is it possible to transfer from one division to another?

11. What is the housing market for single people in _________ _________ (city)? Is public transportation adequate?

12. How much contact and exposure to management is there?

13. How soon should I expect to report to work?

Assessment Questions Asked by Professional Interviewers

1. What goals have you set for yourself? How are you planning to achieve them?

2. Who or what has had the greatest influence on the development of your career interests?

3. What factors did you consider in choosing your major?

4. Why are you interested in our organization?

5. What can you tell me about yourself?

6. What two or three things are most important to you in a position?

7. What kind of work do you want to do?

8. What can you tell me about a project you initiated?

9. What are your expectations of your future employer?

10. What is your GPA? How do you feel about it? Does it reflect your ability?

11. How do you resolve conflicts?

12. What do you feel are your strengths? Your weaknesses? How do you evaluate yourself?

13. What work experience has been the most valuable to you and why?

14. What was the most useful criticism you ever received and who was it from?

15. Can you give an example of a problem you have solved and the process you used?

16. Can you describe the project or situation that best demonstrates your analytical skills?

17. What has been your greatest challenge?

18. Can you describe a situation where you had a conflict with another individual and explain how you dealt with it?

19. What were the biggest problems you have encountered in college? How have you handled them? What did you learn from them?

20. What are your team-player qualities? Give examples.

21. Can you describe your leadership style?

22. What interests or concerns you about the position or the company?

23. In a particular leadership role you had, what was the greatest challenge?

24. What idea have you developed and implemented that was particularly creative or innovative?

25. What characteristics do you think are important for this position?

26. How have your educational and work experiences prepared you for this position?

27. Can you take me through a project where you demonstrated __________________ skills?

28. How do you think you have changed personally since you started college?

29. Can you tell me about a team project of which you are particularly proud and discuss your contribution?

30. How do you motivate people?

31. Why did you choose the extracurricular activities you did? What did you gain? What did you contribute?
32. What types of situations put you under pressure, and how do you deal with the pressure?
33. Can you tell me about a difficult decision you have made?
34. Can you give an example of a situation in which you failed, and explain how you handled it?
35. Can you tell me about a situation when you had to persuade another person of your point of view?
36. What frustrates you the most?
37. Knowing what you know now about your college experience, would you make the same decisions?
38. What can you contribute to this company?
39. How would you react to having your credibility questioned?
40. What characteristics are important in a good manager? How have you displayed one of these characteristics?
41. What challenges are you looking for in a position?
42. Are you willing to relocate or travel as part of your career?
43. What two or three accomplishments have given you the most satisfaction?
44. Can you describe a leadership role of yours and tell why you committed your time to it?
45. How are you conducting your job search, and how will you make your decision?
46. What is the most important lesson you have learned in or out of school?
47. Can you describe a situation where you had to work with someone who was difficult? How was the person difficult, and how did you handle it?
48. We are looking at a lot of great candidates; why are you the best person for this position?
49. How would your friends describe you? Your professors?
50. What else should I know about you?

These questions reflect a significant movement away from standard directive questions towards more open-ended situational cases. Common themes include applications of analytical, problem-solving and decision-making skills; leadership development; creativity; teamwork; and personal development.

After the Interview

1. Write a thank-you note.
2. Call, after a week or two past the expected decision date, if there has been no response from the employer.
3. Record your interview date, the interviewer's name, the company name, and the expected notification response date, etc. for future reference.

WRITING A FOLLOW-UP LETTER

Writing a thank-you letter after an interview is often overlooked, yet many employers believe that the deciding factor between several equitable job candidates has often been the thank-you note. The thank-you letter should be typewritten.

Be sure to write a follow-up letter:

1. After two or three weeks of no reply
2. When a job has been refused
    a. Express your regret that no job is available.
    b. Ask if you might be considered in the future.
3. After an interview
    a. Express your thanks for the interviewer's time and courtesy.
    b. Answer any unanswered questions
    c. Clarify any misconceptions.
4. To accept a job (even if previously done in person or on the phone)
    a. State your acceptance.
    b. Reiterate the agreement—beginning work, etc
    c. Do not start asking favors.
5. To refuse a job offer
    a. Graciously decline the offer.
    b. Be warm and interested.
    c. Indicate that you appreciate the offer.

Be certain that your letters possess the attitude, quality, and skill of a professional.

Follow-up letters are also appropriate after you have received replies to both solicited and unsolicited letters of inquiry, etc.

Writing a Follow-Up Letter After Your Employment Interview

If you are interested in a job that has been discussed in an interview, follow up your meeting with a thank-you letter. The thank-you letter should be directed to the person(s) who interviewed you. Its purpose should be to first thank the interviewer for his time and interest and then to reemphasize the qualities you would bring to the position if hired. In addition to a sincerely stated "thank you" for the interviewer's time and interest, you will want to restate your qualifications for the job in a brief, straightforward manner. Let the interviewer know that you are interested in another meeting. In some cases, you may decide to make a follow-up phone call as well. As in all aspects of a job search, follow-ups must be approached with balance in mind. The point is to let the employer know your skills and enthusiasm without making a pest of yourself. Be attentive to the reaction your letter or phone call elicits and take your cue from there.

In writing a thank-you letter, follow the guidelines shown in Figure 2-5 and the sample shown in Figure 2-6. Note that the thank-you letter should always be typed, be approximately one page long, and consist of three or four paragraphs. If you ask for the business card of each person you talk to, you will know how to correctly spell the individual's name and you will have the person's job title when you prepare your thank-you letter.

Your street address
Your city
Your state and zip code
Date

Interviewer's name
Job title
Company name
Mailing address

Dear Ms./Mr. _________________ :

In the first paragraph, thank the interviewer for her time and interest in meeting with you.

In the second paragraph, mention some of the qualities you think make you a good candidate for the position. You have probably talked about these things during the interview, but this is an opportunity to reemphasize why the employer should hire you.

In the third paragraph, it is a good idea to talk about why you are particularly interested in the employer's organization. Mention some of the reasons you want to work for the organization. Share some of your knowledge about the positive qualities of the company.

In the closing paragraph, say that you look forward to hearing from her in regard to her decision. You can also mention that you would be happy to provide other materials to support your application (transcript, letters of recommendation, samples of your work) and to meet with her again.

Sincerely,

Your name
Area code and phone number

Figure 2-5   *Thank-you letter guidelines*

300 West 14th Avenue
Apartment 1C
St. Louis, Missouri 63021
March 26, 199X

Ms. Annie Wilson
Human Resource Director
J.C. Penney Company
200 East Stemmons Freeway
Dallas, Texas 24031

Dear Ms. Wilson:

Thank you for taking the time to interview me in Dallas on March 21st. It was a pleasure to meet you and the ladies' wear merchandising staff members. In addition, it was a wonderful experience to tour the headquarters of the J.C. Penney Company.

I am extremely interested in the summer internship position we discussed. I believe I possess the qualifications and experience you described during our interview as prerequisites for the job. My employment with Express has provided me with excellent on-the-job training in visual merchandising, receiving, and sales. During my sophomore year at Stephens College, I was able to assist with the production of a major fashion show for an audience of 600 persons. Through a summer internship with J.C. Penney, I could draw upon my background and expand my skills by helping with the promotional efforts of the ladies' wear division. J.C. Penney Company is on the cutting edge of fashion retailing as shown through its recent expansion as well as its future growth plans. To be a member of one of the top retailers in the country would be an exceptional opportunity.

I look forward to hearing from you within the next two weeks. I have enclosed a copy of my resume for your review. If you would like to receive any additional materials to support my application, I would be pleased to forward them to you. My college transcript and a videotape of the fashion show production I assisted with are available at your request. Thank you for your time and consideration.

Sincerely,

Patricia McCoy

Patricia McCoy
(314) 555-7402

Enc.

Figure 2-6 *Example of a thank-you letter*

Getting Settled In

After you have procured your internship position, you can look forward to joining the "real world" work force. On-the-job requirements and expectations are often very different than those of the academic environment. For example, submitting an assignment late in an academic course usually carries the penalty of a lower grade; however, in business, it can mean losing a job or forfeiting a positive reference from an employer. As a student, you may be able sit though a lecture course without participating and pass the course by earning a satisfactory grade. In the industry, your success depends on your positive contributions to the day-to-day activities of the company. A lack of participation in business usually means the lack of continued employment. Below you will find tips to help you succeed in the fast-paced work world of the fashion industry.

ON-THE-JOB TIPS

Your internship experience is designed to help you develop professional work skills. Such experience and skills will increase your opportunities for obtaining a good job after graduation. To be successful in your career also requires developing good personal qualities and work habits. The following guidelines will help you make the most of your internship and increase your job effectiveness.

Present a Positive Attitude

Approach your job with a positive attitude; do not dwell on negative factors or complain about your job, your supervisor, or the company to fellow workers. Not all tasks will be exciting or challenging (which is true of most jobs) and yet, whatever you do, you will find you will still be learning something new. Show enthusiasm and a willingness to pitch in; employers appreciate a cooperative attitude.

Take Initiative

Take an active role in your on-the-job-training. When you have completed your assigned work, do not sit around and wait for another assignment; do the following instead:

1. Ask your supervisor for another project.
2. Offer to assist someone else in the office.
3. Learn as much as you can about your company, its policies, and procedures by reading company literature.
4. Read professional literature in your field. This will identify you as an interested and serious professional.
5. Using good judgment, choose an appropriate time to ask questions of fellow workers and your supervisor regarding the objectives of your department.
6. When you become familiar with the procedures required to perform your job, you may be able to anticipate what the next steps should be. Take the initiative and move on to the next step. Your efforts will save your internship employer time and will increase your value as an employee.

Project Assertiveness

Achieving your goals in a direct, honest, and open manner instead of being either meek or pushy is being assertive. The objectives you will set in your learning agreement are the goals you will be working toward. It is up to you, with guidance and assistance from your supervisor, to attain these goals. Being responsible, using initiative, being flexible, and having a positive attitude are all aspects of assertive behavior.

The following are some situations that may arise during your internship that will require you to speak up for yourself assertively:

You may find you are spending most of your time on routine clerical work instead of performing tasks that would teach you new skills.
Ask your internship employer for additional responsibilities after successfully completing the routine tasks you have been assigned. If you show initiative, accuracy, and speed, the internship employer will often be anxious to have you complete additional work. It is important to keep in mind, however, that there is something to be learned from every job and that the routine clerical work must be done in order for the organization to function.

You may not have enough work to do.
If this situation arises, choose an opportune time to approach your internship employer and explain your concerns. Be clear and specific when stating your problem, not belligerent or whining. If this action is unsuccessful, then speak to your academic internship sponsor. Problems should be handled as early as possible; you do not want to waste half of your internship in an unproductive situation.

You are given an assignment you don't understand.
Never hesitate to ask questions of clarification. It is also important to learn to listen carefully. If you do make a mistake, it is best to admit it rather than to attempt to cover it up.

You have completed several projects and you don't know if your supervisor is satisfied with your performance.

As part of your professional growth, you will want to know how you are performing. Ask your supervisor for feedback if it is not volunteered. When you receive feedback, listen carefully without responding defensively. Take this as an opportunity to grow and learn.

Develop Professional Conduct and Work Habits

To gain the respect of your employer, keep in mind the following:

1. Make sure that you arrive at work on time. Lateness or absence is excusable only if you are physically ill or have a serious personal emergency. If for these reasons you will be detained from work, call your supervisor immediately and keep him apprised of your status and your expected return to work. School holidays are not necessarily work holidays.

2. Observe how professional staff members in your organization dress and use that as your guideline. Some organizations have more rigid standards than others. Regardless of your taste in dress, some degree of conformity is expected.

3. Keep a notebook. It is difficult to remember everything that your supervisor and others tell you, so put it all in writing. This will also help you manage your time and set work priorities. Record names and phone numbers of people you meet; some of these contacts may be helpful to you in the future.

4. If you cannot complete an assigned task on time, make sure you let your supervisor know. Be realistic about your limitations and the number of assignments you can undertake.

5. If you produce a project, write an article, or the like, ask your supervisor for a copy for your own files. This may be useful to you when you are looking for a job.

Five Rules for the Workplace

1. **Work a full day, every day.** You are expected to be on the job during working hours. Working late does not make up for arriving late, especially if your boss needs something done at 8 a.m. Do not call in sick unless you have to. Missing a day of work is more serious than missing a class. Missing work time will not only displease your supervisor; it may make your hardworking coworkers resentful, as well.

2. **Get your work done on time.** In school, you may be able to turn papers in late, but finishing work assignments after the deadline is unacceptable. Excuses do not help. If you are having trouble completing an assignment, tell your supervisor as soon as possible so that she can call in reinforcements.

3. **Your boss is your boss.** Be respectful and follow orders. When you feel you have special insight that can help solve a problem, by all means, speak up. However, do not argue over the small items, or you may irritate your boss and get a reputation as a complainer.

4. **No job is fun all the time.** Every job has its share of tedium and frustration. It stands to reason that the newest and least experienced employees will be asked to complete many of the routine tasks. Do not be discouraged. Do your best, as cheerfully as possible, and watch for opportunities. Your chance for a plum assignment will come.

5. **Be honest.** Everybody makes mistakes. Do not be afraid to own up to yours. Lying or laying the blame on someone else can be damaging to your career, as well as your conscience.

Ten Tips for Success

1. Know where your job fits in the organization.
2. Put your efforts into the tasks that your boss values. You earn an A when you please your boss, not necessarily when you do what you think is important.
3. Do not be afraid to ask questions, and learn where to go for answers.
4. Let other people know when you have done a good job. Being good isn't enough; people have to know you are good.
5. Learn to communicate effectively—and to the right people.

6. Always share credit; never share blame.
7. Stay cool and reasonable. Do not let your emotions control your actions.
8. Be sensitive to office politics.
9. Remember the importance of networking.
10. Learn how to manage stress *before* the need arises.

Changing Your Internship Plans

Your internship is a job and differs from your other academic courses in many ways. It is a professional relationship and, once you have begun your internship, you may not withdraw from it in the same way that you would from another academic course. If there is an extraordinary circumstance, you will need to discuss the specific situation with your academic sponsor in order to receive approval to withdraw from the assigned internship position. Examples of extraordinary circumstances include: illness (yours or the internship employer's); a drastic change in your internship organization, such as a merger or the elimination of your business; or an employee transfer that relocates your direct employer, leaving you with a new internship supervisor who is unwilling to commit to your internship requirements. Your academic sponsor will confer with you (and possibly the internship employer) to assure that every effort has been made to fulfill the requirements of your original Employer/Student/Academic Sponsor Agreement (Appendix A).

Similarly, changing internships, once you have begun, can only be done if it is clear that all efforts have been made to resolve any problems. For example, you may have made arrangements to complete your internship in the children's wear division of a department store. It is not permissible for you to change divisions without approval of your academic internship sponsor. In some cases, the original Employer/Student/Academic Sponsor Agreement will specify that you will work in a wide range of departments; but if it does not, you will need to obtain approval from your academic sponsor to alter the original agreement.

Your Internship Evaluation

Your internship employer will review you formally at the conclusion of your internship work experience through a written evaluation form available in Appendix C. It is a good idea to take the time to review the evaluation form often during the internship. This helps you to keep in mind the qualities the internship employer will be critiquing as he reflects on your performance at the end of the work experience. Your academic internship sponsor will then assess your employer evaluation, review your written responses in *A Guide to Analyzing Your Fashion Industry Internship,* and calculate a final grade for your academic internship credit.

OTHER PRACTICAL CONSIDERATIONS

In addition to your internship itself, other practical considerations must be taken into account.

Housing

If you choose to complete your internship in a location away from home, you will need to secure a place to stay. It is your responsibility to find housing, not your employer's. While your employer may have some great suggestions for housing and you should not be afraid to ask, you should assume responsibility for action. Students have previously found the following solutions to internship housing:

1. **Colleges/Universities**—This is often the best alternative. Find the residential college located near your internship location and contact the Student Life Office for short-term housing options and prices. Sometimes the college will require a letter of introduction from the academic internship sponsor.
2. **Graduates of Your Institution**—You may decide to write to alumni soliciting housing suggestions. Be certain to include the dates and exact location of your employment situation. Students have successfully exchanged child care, house-sitting, etc. for free board.
3. **Other**—These may include friends of the family, religious contacts, student friends and their parents.

Transportation

Remember to check out the buses, taxicabs, subway systems, and car rental options in your internship location. You may be able to walk or ride a bicycle to work. If not, however, you will want to include transportation costs as part of your internship expense budget.

Budgeting

It is important to plan ahead regarding any expenses that may be associated with your internship experience. Travel to and from the internship location, lodging and related utilities, deposits for phone and utilities, meals, ground transportation, telephone bills, and clothing expenses are some of the costs you may incur.

Dressing for Success

Some companies will require you to wear clothing produced or sold by their own establishments; they often offer substantial discounts on their merchandise to enable employees to dress accordingly. For example, employees of Express retail outlets and Esprit apparel manufacturer are requested to wear merchandise sold by their respective firms. Some businesses have a formal dress code, possibly requiring suits, while others encourage casual dress, possibly jeans and tennis shoes.

You may not be able to make a judgment call on appropriate apparel for your position based solely on your observations during the interview process. While the sales personnel and the receptionist in an apparel manufacturer's showroom may be dressed in sophisticated sportswear, the pattern makers and sample hands in the adjacent factory may be wearing slacks and comfortable shoes. Your attire choice often depends on your particular position within the company. Before you purchase clothing or pack your suitcase for your internship work experience, it is entirely appropriate to ask your internship contact person to describe the firm's dress preference in relationship to your work assignments.

Other factors to consider when determining your work wardrobe are weather conditions, "off-duty" clothing needs, and the variety of job requirements. If your internship is with an apparel manufacturer, for example, you may be required to work in the factory some days, sell in the showroom other days, and entertain clients with the manufacturers' representative in the evenings.

Remember, this is the fashion industry and your appearance makes a significant impression.

Nature of the Organization

Basically, organizations may be categorized by seven classifications: form of organization, ownership, types of merchandise sold, extent of non-store selling, types of services offered, extent of departmentalization, and communication channels. Some retail organizations may fall into more than one category. For example, J.C. Penney Company maintains department stores and operates a mail order catalogue business.

ORGANIZATION CLASSIFICATIONS

In the following sections, each of the seven classifications of organizations will be discussed.

Legal Forms of Organizations

A business may be classified under three types of legal organization: sole proprietorship, partnership, or corporation. In a **sole proprietorship**, one person owns the business and assumes personal responsibility for its debts. In a **partnership**, two or more people invest their time and money while maintaining liability for business debts. On the basis of a partnership contract, the owners agree on how the business is to be operated, the amount of time each partner will devote to it, and how profits and losses will be shared. Within a **corporation**, stockholders invest in the business but do not necessarily share in management decisions. Major decisions are made by a board of directors, while daily operations are conducted by executives and employees of the organization. Stockholders have limited personal responsibility for the firm's debts, as determined by the amount of their investments.

Describe the legal form of organization for your internship organization. Include the name of the firm, company location (headquarters and branch divisions), and auxiliary divisions of the firm, if applicable.

____

____

____

____

____

Ownership

Ownership of businesses may take several forms of legal organization. The sole proprietor may own a chain store; the corporation may own a franchise. The way control of an organization is exercised may be classified as follows:

1. **Chain operations** are multiple outlets under common ownership whose major functions (buying, advertising, employment) are often controlled by a central headquarters (e.g., Walmart, Sears).

2. An **ownership group** is a parent corporation that owns divisions of a business (e.g., Federated, Dayton Hudson, Carter Hawley Hale).

3. **Manufacturer/retailers** operate their own outlets, eliminating wholesalers and gaining absolute control of the distribution process (e.g., Kinney Shoes).
4. **Independently-owned** businesses usually have only one outlet, often owner-managed (e.g., My Sister's Circus, Columbia, Missouri).
5. **Leased departments** are arrangements in which a retailer rents space within his store to another company (e.g., Estee Lauder).
6. A **franchise** is a manufacturer, wholesaler, or service company that sells a smaller firm or individual the right to conduct a business in a specified manner within a certain period of time, using the franchise organization's name, logo, etc. (e.g., Merle Norman Cosmetics).
7. In a **consumer cooperative association**, consumers own shares in the operation. While owners determine business policy, actual operations are maintained by a manager (e.g., University Supermarket, Columbia, Missouri).

Describe the type of ownership of your internship organization. List executives responsible for ownership functions.

____

____

____

____

____

____

____

____

____

____

Types of Merchandise Sold

Types of merchandise sold are examined in Chapters 8 and 9.

Extent of Nonstore Selling

Nonstore selling methods do not require the physical plant, yet are viable components that contribute to the productivity of many textile and apparel operations. For example, the owner of a lingerie boutique may develop a party plan to present the store's merchandise in the consumer's home. A specialty store may produce a catalogue to mail to current and prospective customers. Nonstore selling methods are categorized as direct selling, party plans, mail order retailing, catalogue retailing, telephone selling, and electronic selling. The home shopping network of QVC illustrates nonstore selling via television. Nonstore selling suggests alternative channels of distribution, which are discussed more extensively in Chapter 11.

Describe the extent of nonstore selling used by your internship organization. If none have been implemented, explain why nonstore selling techniques are not applicable or suggest types of nonstore selling that may improve profitability of the internship organization.

Types of Services Offered

Some organizations sell *services* rather than tangible products. Categories of services sold are: rentals; repairs, maintenance and custom work; or personal services. Formal attire and costume rental, alteration service, custom sewing, wardrobe consultation, and fashion show production are examples of services sold by textile and apparel firms. While some businesses are totally service-oriented (resident buying office), others provide some service for a fee.

Describe the extent of services sold by your internship organization.

____

____

____

____

____

____

____

Extent of Departmentalization

Many medium-sized and large department stores are organized according to various retailing functions. Many apparel manufacturers, fashion forecasting services, resident buying offices, and related mid- to large-sized fashion businesses are organized in a similar manner. Paul Mazur developed the original concept of "planning by functions" in 1927. The **Mazur Plan** divided business activities into four major areas: merchandising, public relations, operations, and control. Later, the National Retail Merchants' Association (now called the National Retail Federation) added fifth and sixth functions, personnel and branch division. **Merchandising** includes responsibility for all the activities involved in buying and selling merchandise. **Public relations** is concerned with all nonpersonal selling activities (sales promotions, advertising, and publicity). The major activities of operations are business maintenance, purchasing of supplies and equipment to operate the business, customer services, and security. The **control** division is responsible for monitoring the firm's financial status through accounting and record keeping, credit and collections, budgeting, and inventory control. The **personnel** area is responsible for overseeing the company's human resources, the employees of the organization. Finally, the **branch division** takes responsibility for the organization's outlets that are not within the company's headquarters.

Although small, independent businesses perform many of the same functions as large retailers, the organization structure is simpler as each employee is often responsible for several functions. Each function will be explored in depth on the following pages.

The Operations Function All functions related to the physical operation of the organization are grouped together under the supervision of the manager, superintendent, or director of organization operations. The major activities of the operations management function are physical plant maintenance, purchasing of supplies and equipment, customer service, and security. In addition, **operations management** includes receiving, marking, and checking of merchandise receipts; warehouse distribution; and shipping of merchandise.

List the responsibilities of your organization's operations manager.

____

____

____

____

____

____

Annually, retailers and manufacturers lose millions of dollars to shoplifting, internal theft, and clerical errors. These losses are referred to as **shrinkages** or **shortages**, the difference between a book inventory and an actual physical inventory. **Loss prevention** is the process of preventing merchandise loss by deterring illegal activities such as shoplifting and employee theft.

If your internship organization is a retail operation, clerical errors, shoplifting, and employee pilferage are loss prevention concerns. If you are employed by an apparel manufacturing firm, internal and external theft can affect profits. If you are working with the costume collection of a museum, theft can directly affect the quality and quantity of the collection.

Discuss the loss prevention philosophy of your internship organization. What is the firm's existing shortage percent? Goal shortage percent?

____

____

____

____

Describe the physical or structural deterrents to shortages/losses used by your internship organization (e.g., security systems). Also, discuss techniques used to discourage shoplifting if you are employed by a retail firm.

____

____

____

____

____

____

Discuss techniques used by your organization to discourage employee pilferage.

____

____

____

____

____

____

____

Summarize techniques used by your organization to reduce employee clerical errors.

Who provides instruction to employees regarding loss prevention techniques?

The Merchandising Function   The major responsibility of the merchandising function is to maintain the inventory offered for sale in accordance with the requirements of the consumer. It can be evaluated by comparing the stock of goods offered for sale with consumer need.

Describe written plans required before the buyer may begin purchasing merchandise. What preparations are made by the manufacturers' representative or apparel manufacturer before presenting the merchandise to the buyers?

____

____

____

____

____

____

Discuss types of merchandise sources used by your internship organization. For each source, allocate its approximate percentages of the merchandise mix. Consider the following sources:

- **Key** *versus* **secondary vendors**
- **Direct** *versus* **wholesale purchasing**
- **Private label** *versus* **national brand sources**
- **Resident buying office** *versus* **organization**
- **Foreign** *versus* **domestic manufacturers**
- **Promotional** *versus* **regular-priced sources**

____

____

____

____

____

____

____

____

____

How are merchandise sources selected? Who approves acceptance of a new source? What factors does the buyer take into consideration? If your internship organization is a manufacturers' representative, how does he select and solicit new lines to represent? Please provide examples of new resources used by the firm.

____

____

____

____

____

____

____

____

____

____

Where are the merchandise sources located? Does the buyer travel to merchandise sources or meet with source representatives in the internship organization offices? Does the manufacturers' representative travel to retail accounts and/or regional markets? List locations and dates of regional markets and trade shows attended by buyers (or manufacturers' representatives if this is your internship segment) of the internship organization. How do the various markets compare? If your internship employer is a manufacturers' representative or a manufacturer, how is a representative's sales territory determined? If applicable, please define the geographical specifics of the rep's territory.

____

____

____

____

____

____

____

____

____

Examine normal discount terms for merchandise purchased by your organization. Describe available promotional aids, if applicable.

List top-performing merchandise sources by merchandise classification. Note why each source is a high performer.

According to the categories below, analyze the merchandising policies developed by your internship organization to provide a framework for the firm's buying and selling activities:

- *Fashion leadership (**product life cycle** position)*
- ***Basic stock** vs. **fashion goods***
- *Merchandise quality*
- *Assortment **depth** and **breadth***
- ***Exclusivity***

____

____

____

____

____

____

____

____

Personnel Function   Human resource management (the personnel division) is concerned with hiring, training, motivating, and understanding the needs of employees in order to develop a productive work force. The human resource division functions include:

1. Recruiting and hiring new employees
2. Training and retraining current employees
3. Working with personnel transfers, promotions, and discharges
4. Establishing wage and compensation scales
5. Creating and managing employee fringe benefits

How does your organization locate qualified applicants for managerial and non-managerial positions?

____

____

____

____

____

____

____

Describe the steps used by your organization to select position applicants. Also, discuss any employment tests that are utilized.

____

Discuss training offered by human resources management for organization employees. If you are interning with a manufacturers' representative, for example, how does she receive training regarding selling a product line(s) from the manufacturer(s)? Sales meetings? Literature? How frequently is training conducted?

How is the demand for employees projected? Who is responsible for forecasting future employment needs?

If your internship organization has an executive (management) training program, describe it.

____

____

____

____

____

____

____

____

Summarize types of discounts and benefits available to employees of your internship organization.

____

____

____

____

____

____

How does your organization evaluate employee productivity? Are sales quotas provided?

____

____

____

____

____

____

Describe the frequency and depth of employee performance reviews. Who directs employee performance reviews?

The Control Function Usually under the supervision of the controller or treasurer, the control function is charged with safeguarding the company's financial status. The control function delegates responsibilities into three areas:

Accounting	Control	Credit
general accounting	expense control	invoicing customers
accounts payable	budget control	cashiers in credit office
insurance and taxes	sales audit	charge accounts
incoming mail	merchandise	credit authorization
payroll	statistics &	credit interviews
	reports	deferred payments
	inventory planning	
	& supervision reports	

Accounting and record keeping, credit and collections, budgeting, and inventory control are the primary responsibilities of the control function.

Describe the location, departmentalization, and procedures of the control function of your internship organization.

Discuss types of credit offered by your internship organization.

Explain the use of computers in the control function (e.g., inventory control, credit management, payroll, etc.).

The Public Relations Function This division is concerned with all nonpersonal selling activities. Major activities of the public relations function are advertising, publicity, visual merchandising, and promotion planning for the entire organization. The public relations function is thoroughly discussed in Chapter 12.

An overview of public relations includes discussion of the organization's projected personality or image. Public relations is used to project the character of the organization to the consumer and to the community. Often, conflicting images result. For example, a retailer may believe he is offering fashion-forward merchandise and excellent customer services. The consumer may perceive the store's merchandise as "conservative" and customer services as inadequate due to a lack of delivery and alteration services. The community may view this retailer with high regard as he contributes generously to local charities. It is often difficult for the organization's management to objectively analyze consumer and community perceptions.

Discuss the organization's personality as it is viewed by:

1. the organization itself

____

____

____

____

____

____

2. the consumer it serves

____

____

____

____

____

____

3. the community or communities in which it is located

____

____

____

____

____

____

In what ways does your organization project its personality through public relations efforts? If public relations are unexamined by your internship organization, please create an effective public relations plan for your company.

____

____

____

____

____

____

____

____

____

____

____

____

____

____

The Organizational Structure Figures 4-1 and 4-2 indicate common organizational structures for small and large retailing operations and apparel manufacturing companies.

List personnel names and titles and indicate job responsibilities for each position within your internship organization. If your internship organization's structure is not represented by Figure 4-1 or Figure 4-2, use the following page to chart the organizational structure. Show the corporate organizational structure and branch organizational structure, if applicable.

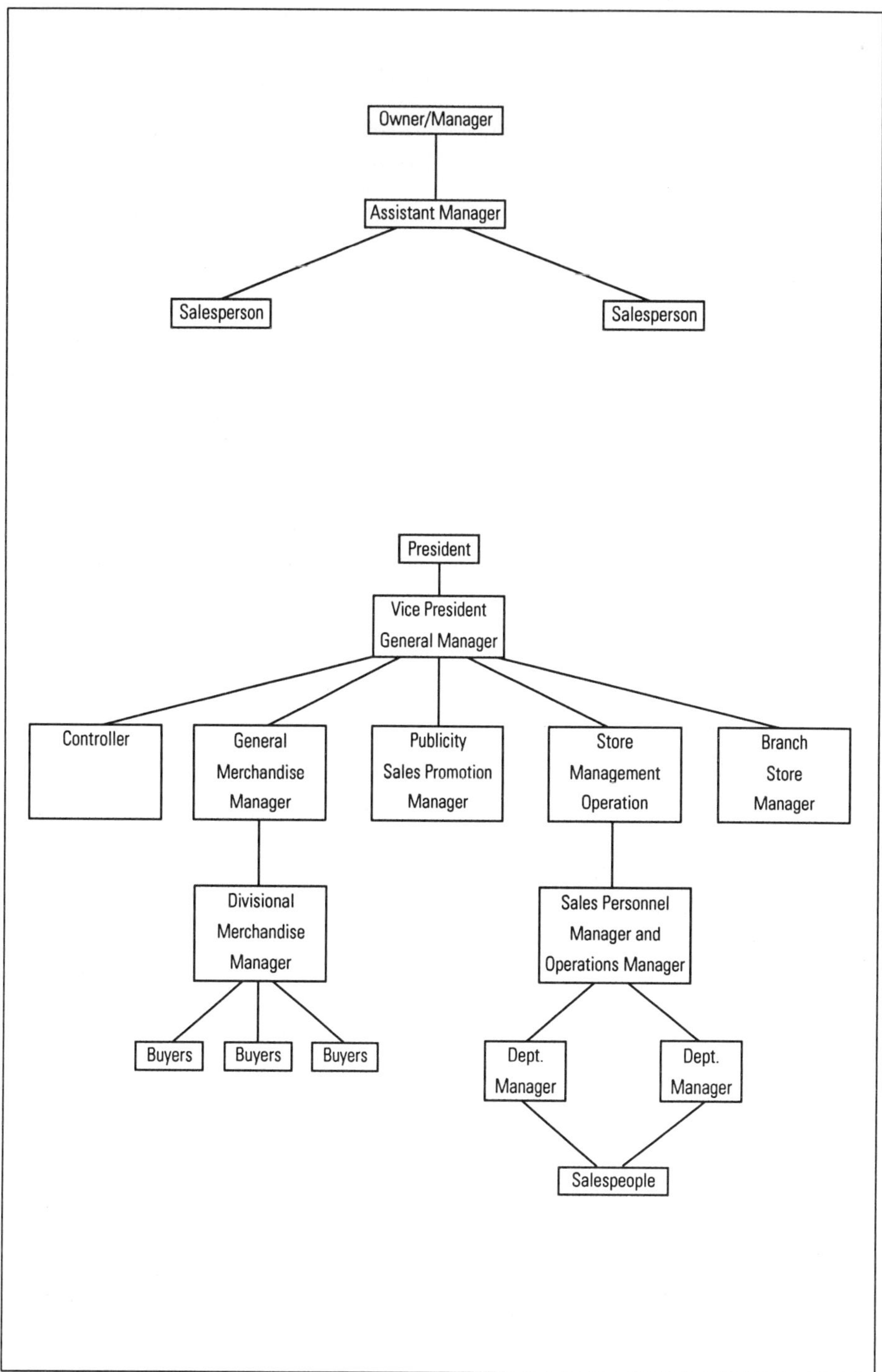

Figure 4-1 *Common organizational structure for small and large retailing organizations*

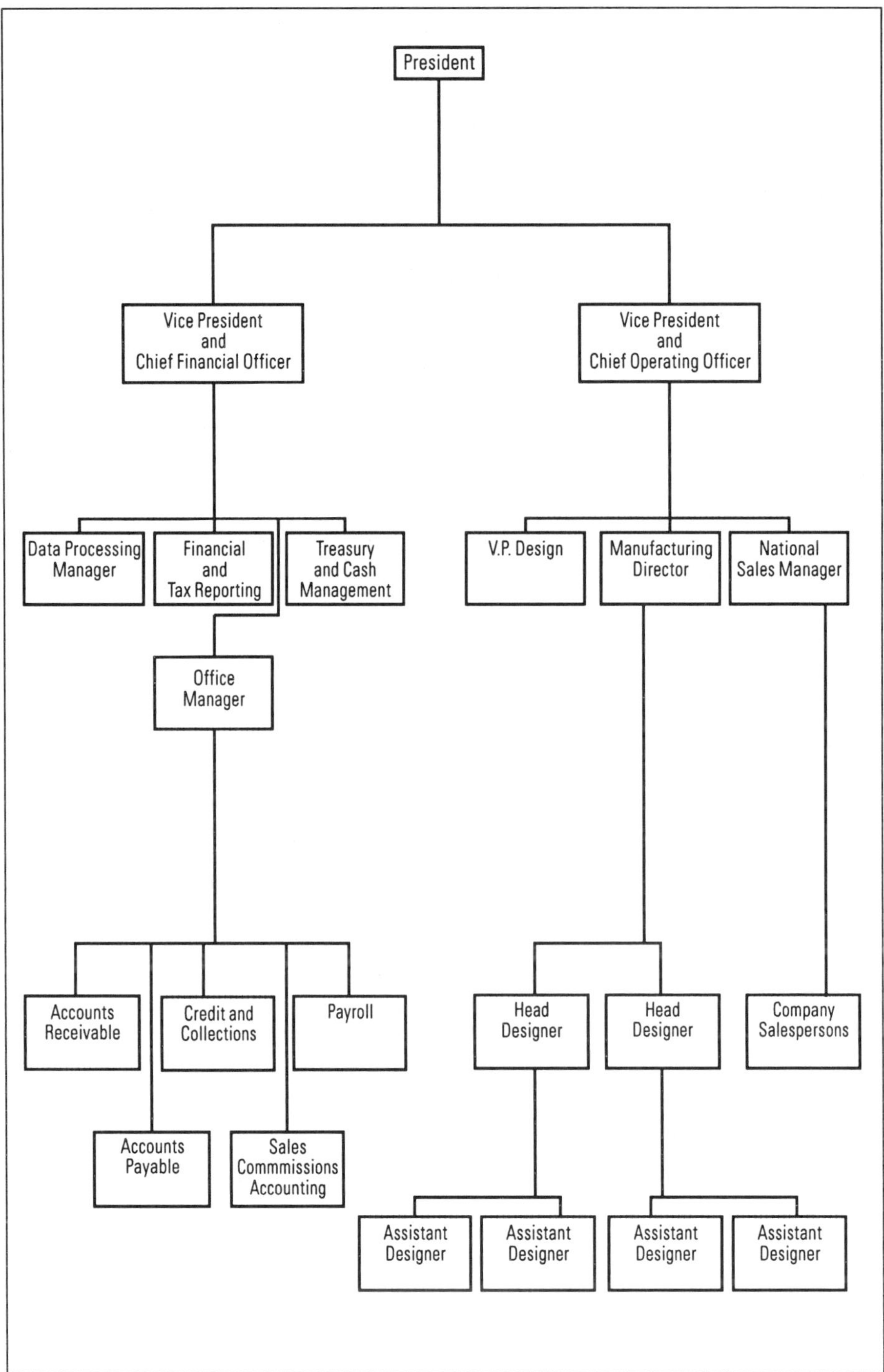

Figure 4-2 *Common organizational structure for an apparel manufacturing comapny*

YOUR INTERNSHIP ORGANIZATIONAL STRUCTURE DIAGRAM

Organization Communications Channels Effective communication assists management with recognition of employee and consumer wants and needs. It also helps employees understand organizational objectives, policies, and opportunities. Commonly used channels of communication are **downward vertical** (manager to employee), **upward vertical** (employee to manager), and **horizontal** (manager to manager).

Informal Communication is the use of vertical and horizontal lines for verbal communication. An unofficial communication network is referred to as a grapevine, usually transporting messages (although often distorted) faster than through official channels. **Formal communication** involves the use of employee handbooks, suggestion systems, newsletters, bulletins, meetings, and education departments (formerly called training departments).

Provide examples of formal and informal communication methods used by your internship organization. Diagram the examples to illustrate downward vertical, upward vertical, or horizontal communication channels.

The Customer

Most organizations will succeed or fail according to their ability to analyze and understand the customer. The customer's psyche, emotional needs, habits, and purchasing motives internally influence spending patterns. Economic factors, income, age, and location also contribute to customer behavior. An organization's ability to develop a sound strategy for pleasing the customer requires both constant evaluation of the customer as well as the ability to influence customer behavior.

BUYING MOTIVES

Buying motives, or needs or desires that cause the customer to act or buy include:

1. **Emotional**—motives developed without logical thinking (love, vanity)
2. **Rational**—motives involving judgment and logical thinking (security, durability)

3. **Biogenic**—motives relating to physical needs (food, sex)
4. **Psychogenic**—motives stemming from psychological needs (to enhance the ego, to protect)
5. **Patronage**—reasons why consumers choose one place to shop rather than another

Describe the buying motives used by your internship organization to increase productivity.

____

____

____

____

____

____

THE CUSTOMER DECISION PROCESS

The **buying process** consists of steps the consumer goes through when deciding what, when, where, and how to buy. The steps in the consumer decision process are: (1) recognition of a need, (2) search for information, (3) evaluation, (4) purchase decision, and (5) post-purchase behavior.

Describe the buying process steps in detail, using a particular product of your internship organization as an example.

Demographics and Market Segmentation

Demographics refers to the breakdown of the population into statistical categories such as age, gender, education, occupation, income, households, and marital status. Organizations that are interested in reaching special populations are concerned with **market segmentation,** the process of dividing the total market into smaller homogenous sections. Organizations look for several things in segmenting markets. Consumer groups are chosen that are as similar as possible in their merchandise preferences, tastes, and shopping habits. A segment of the market with long-term potential that is not effectively served by competition is sought by organizations developing a market segment. Important market segments include working women, customers with special needs, minority groups, and the elderly.

Lifestyles

Lifestyles are affected by demographic background because age, income, and education greatly influence the way a person may choose to live. A lifestyle is the unique way in which a particular group sets itself apart from others. An analysis of consumer lifestyles requires the examination of social class, reference groups, and cultural influences.

Social Classes

Social classes are homogeneous divisions of families and individuals within a society. A social class division is determined by occupation, source of income, education, family background, dwelling type, and other variables. Six levels of the class system are upper-upper, lower-upper, upper-middle, lower-middle, upper-lower and lower-lower.

Reference Groups

Groups that are influential in shaping attitudes and opinions are known as **reference groups.** The family is considered one of the most influential of all reference groups. The members of reference groups who exert influence on consumer decision making are called **opinion leaders.** Opinion leaders are found on all social levels and are selected by their followers for several reasons: they are regarded as a source of information and advice, possess recognized expertise, are highly visible to the group, and are first to adopt new styles.

Culture

Culture and lifestyles are inseparable. **Culture** refers to the behavior typical of a group or class. The social meaning attached to a product within a culture is critical in assessing how the product might be accepted. Religious beliefs, economic relations, and nationality or heritage are several key aspects of culture. The work ethic, a need for security, and a drive for status spark the competitive drive to purchase products that are identified with success, such as designer apparel and fine jewelry.

Describe the consumer profile of the internship organization. Include demographics, lifestyles, social classes, reference groups, and cultural influences. If your internship experience is with an apparel manufacturer or a manufacturer's representative, describe the consumer profile in two ways: the retail operation as a consumer (the store that purchases the merchandise) and the ultimate consumer (the person who ultimately uses the goods).

The Company Mission

The members of a business organization can coordinate their individual efforts in a united direction through the development of a company mission statement and a plan describing the company's objectives and goals.

THE MISSION STATEMENT

An organization develops formal **mission statements** to answer four questions: (1) What is the existing business? (2) Who is the customer? (3) What is value to the customer? (4) What potential opportunities exist? An effective mission statement motivates company personnel through a shared sense of direction, opportunity, significance, and achievement. Under the company mission statement, widely dispersed employees can work independently yet collectively toward realizing the organization's potential. The mission statement should define the business domain(s) in which the organization will operate in terms of products, technologies, customer groups, customer needs, etc.

A mission statement can be as long as a paragraph or as short as a single sentence. An example of the former is the mission statement developed for a specific committee of the Women's Network Organization, a business women's organization affiliated with the Chamber of Commerce:

- "The mission of the Women's Network Business Managers Committee is to provide a means of communication in an informal setting for business managers and supervisors. The committee gives women the opportunity to exchange ideas and discuss problems, solutions, and techniques."

An example of the latter is the following sentence that has been the guiding force for Nordstrom over nine decades of operation:

- "Nordstrom remains committed to its founding principles of providing its customers with the best possible quality, value, service, and selection."

Discuss the mission statement of your internship organization. If the organization has not developed a formal mission statement, compose one to define the business domain(s). Within the mission statement, please answer questions 1 through 4, as listed above.

COMPANY OBJECTIVES AND GOALS

The mission statement is turned into a detailed set of supporting objectives for each level of management. These objectives should be turned into specific quantitative goals to obtain planning and control, such as "increase market share to 20% by the end of the year." Goals describe objectives that have been made specific with respect to magnitude and time.

For example, The Fashion Group International, Inc., a non-profit organization for industry professionals, established the following goals for 1994 for its membership of over 6,000 women in the fashion industry and related fields:

- To advance professionalism in fashion and its related lifestyle industries, with a particular emphasis on the role and development of women.
- To provide a public forum for examination of important contemporary issues in fashion and the business of fashion.
- To present timely information regarding national and global trends that have an effect on the fashion industries.
- To attain greater recognition for women's achievements in business.
- To encourage women to seek career opportunities in fashion and related industries.
- To provide activities and programs that enhance networking skills and encourage interpersonal contacts so as to further the professional, social, and personal development of members.
- To administer the activities of The Fashion Group International Foundation.

Discuss the objectives and goals of your internship organization. If goals and objectives have not been specified by management of the organization, please originate them for the current year.

____

____

____

____

____

____

____

____

____

____

____

As an exercise to maximize your internship experience, establish specific goals and objectives for yourself within your internship. Keep in mind that these should obviously parallel those of the business organization and reflect the requirements of your internship for college credit.

____

____

____

____

____

____

____

MARKET POSITIONING

Market positioning refers to arranging for a product to occupy a clear, distinctive, and desirable place in the market and in the minds of target customers. When positioning itself in a market segment, an organization will identify all the competitive products and brands currently serving customers. Organizations seek out marketing opportunities in which the firm would enjoy a competitive advantage.

Sears, Roebuck, and Co. recently repositioned itself through a major restructuring program that enabled the company to concentrate on its retail and insurance businesses. A primary repositioning effort was the conversion of about 350 former catalog sales stores to new, small retail stores that are operated by independent dealers. Other repositioning steps included discontinuing its U.S. catalog operations, closing unprofitable U.S. retail and specialty stores (among them, Pinstripes Petites), streamlining or discontinuing various unprofitable activities, and offering a voluntary early retirement program to certain salaried associates. This repositioning program is expected to improve net income by about $300 million annually.

Describe any positioning/repositioning strategies attempted by your internship organization.

____

____

____

____

____

____

THE COMPETITIVE ENVIRONMENT

Every organization faces a wide range of competitors. An organization must understand direct competitors while recognizing that there are other ways of competing to satisfy the customer's needs. For example, the specialty store may directly compete with other local specialty stores. However, it is indirectly competing with discount operations, home sewing firms, and department stores.

List the direct and indirect competitors for your internship organization.

____

____

____

____

Complete the following competitor survey form (Figure 6-1) using a direct competitor. (Some items may not be applicable to a competitor of your internship organization.)

+ = above average
x = average
− = below average
? = not applicable

Organization ________________________ Department _______________________

Address ________________________ Date/Day/Time _______________________

LOCATION & FACILITIES	+	x	−	?	COMMENTS:
1. "affinity" of location					
2. accessibility					
3. parking					
4. general appearance of building					
5. interior decor					
6. maintenance / cleanliness					
MERCHANDISE & PRICE					
7. emphasis given to price					
8. general quality of merchandise					
9. quality at low price range					
10. quality at mid price range					
11. quality at high price range					
12. national brands carried					
13. marked-down/sale merchandise					
14. general breadth of assortment					
15. general depth of assortment					

Figure 6-1 *Competitor survey*

SALES & PROMOTION	+	x	–	?	COMMENTS:
16. quality of personal selling					
17. quality of advertising					
18. quality of window displays					
19. quality of interior displays					
20. quality of promotion events					

GENERAL COMMENTS

21.   Describe the traffic or business level of the organization (e.g., number of potential customers in the building at the time of your observation).

____

____

____

____

____

22.   Discuss the level of the organization's services.

____

____

____

____

23.   Profile the customer group in the business at the time of your visit.

____

____

____

____

Figure 6-1 *Competitor survey*

24. Summarize your overall impressions of the company and its operations.

25. Describe other observations, unusual happenings, "attention-getters," etc.

Figure 6-1 *Competitor survey*

The External Environment

No organization operates in a vacuum. Rather, there are many influences and events positioned outside the organization that affect its life. These influences and events are sometimes referred to as the **external** or **macroenvironment** of the organization. Because these influences and events cannot be controlled by the management of the organization, they are sometimes called **uncontrollable variables.** Although these variables are uncontrollable, management must be constantly sensitive to them in terms of how they affect the organization, and therefore result in patterns of decision making.

The macroenvironment is often broken down into subsets for discussion and analysis. These subsets include: 1. the economic environment, 2. the social environment, 3. the political/legal environment, 4. the natural environment, 5. the technological environment, and 6. the competitive environment. Because the competitive environment is addressed thoroughly in Chapter 7, it will not be examined here. Each of these environments affects organizations in the textile/apparel industry, but in different ways and to differing degrees, depending on where that organization is in the channel of distribution and how that organization relates to its clients. A closer look at each of these subsets makes this clear.

THE ECONOMIC ENVIRONMENT

A single organization cannot do anything about the general economic state of the world, the nation, or the local community, nor can it do anything about the policy decisions of the National Reserve. But these certainly affect the economic life—in fact the whole life—of the organization. The important question is, "How do changes in the economy and economic policy affect the organization?" Can you assume that a depressed economic environment will be bad for all retailers, for example? While general merchandise retailers may suffer under such circumstances, others (such as do-it-yourself retailers or those selling home sewing merchandise) may thrive as never before.

In what ways has the economic environment recently affected your specific organization? How does the economic environment affect organizations in your industry segment in general? In addition, discuss the current economic environment.

____

____

____

THE SOCIAL ENVIRONMENT

Changes in population growth, geographical residence patterns, attitudes about having children, attitudes about appropriate gender roles and age-appropriate behaviors, and changing commitments to religious expression are all things that make up the social environment. Of course, there are many others. A social shift toward increased education might result in a larger market for a museum. An increase in the number of professional working women might result in a men's furnishings store experiencing great success by the addition of a line of women's tailored suits and accessories. A trend toward smaller family size by two income families might alter spending patterns that have repercussions all the way back down the channel of distribution to retailer, manufacturer, and designer.

What changes in the social environment have recently affected the life of your specific organization? To what extent are the decision makers in your organization sensitive to these changes and their impact? In general, how have social changes affected organization in your industry segment?

____

____

____

____

____

____

____

____

____

THE POLITICAL/LEGAL ENVIRONMENT

The overthrow of a South American government, import quotas on merchandise manufactured in the Orient, the prevailing attitude of the courts on acquisitions and mergers, a local community's change in laws regarding Sunday openings—these are only a few of the issues that comprise the political/legal environment in business. For example, a 1984 U.S. Customs decision to interpret the quota law resulted in a battle over imported garments between apparel retailers and manufacturers.

In what ways is your organization affected by the political/legal environment? In what ways are organizations in your industry segment affected?

____

____

____

____

____

____

____

____

____

____

____

____

THE NATURAL ENVIRONMENT

All of those things that homeowners' insurance does not cover are among the elements that comprise the natural environment: wind, water, etc. More subtle and more gradual are issues such as the erosion of top soil from prime agricultural land—which, of course, affects the production of cotton and the production of some man-made fibers as well. Cold weather is generally believed to lead to depressed sales, but the effect is not just on the behavior of customers; it also includes late shipments, etc. The concern over the world's supply of oil and the so-called "oil crisis" has a dramatic impact on the production of most man-made fibers, energy costs in factories and stores, and how far customers are willing to drive to get a bargain.

In what ways is your organization affected by the natural environment? In what ways are organizations in your industry segment affected?

____

____

____

____

____

____

____

____

____

____

____

____

THE TECHNOLOGICAL ENVIRONMENT

The computer has revolutionized all segments of the textile/apparel industry, from retailing to design, and has altered the way information is transmitted and used, how patterns are designed and graded, and how accounts are maintained. New materials aid costume restoration; new low-soiling carpets reduce cleaning expenses; new manufacturing equipment results in changes in labor costs and in employee morale within the organization. Technological advances affect businesses throughout the distribution channel.

A more mundane example was the 7th Avenue Blackout in New York City. During a major market week in Manhattan, the electricity was unexpectedly shut off in all of the major market buildings. There were no lights, escalators and elevators did not function, and security was a major concern. The power failure sent buyers scurrying from Manhattan to the regional markets nearest their store locations. The primary result was a positive economic outcome for the manufacturers' representatives in the regional markets and a disaster for those representatives in the New York showrooms.

In what ways is your organization affected by the technological environment? In what ways are organizations in your industry segment affected?

Product Identification

A **product** is anything offered to a market for attention, acquisition, use, or consumption. A product is capable of satisfying a consumer's want or need and may be an object, service, activity, person, place, organization, or idea.

PRODUCT LEVELS

There are three levels of a product:

1. **Core**—main benefit or service
2. **Formal**—includes packaging, brand name, quality, styling, and features.
3. **Augmented**—includes installation, delivery, credit, after-sale service, warranty, advertising, and promotion.

As an example, Mary Kay offers cosmetic items (lipstick, cleanser, eye shadow, etc.) as its core product. The lipstick tube and applicator, package, color assortment, and brand name are parts of the formal level of its product. Finally, attention to customers, complimentary facial service, and home delivery are elements of its augmented product level. If you are working for a service-oriented business, the product *is* the service. For example, a hair salon may feature hair styling, makeup application, and nail care as its products.

Identify and describe the product levels of your internship organization.

Formal:____

____

____

____

____

Augmented: ____

____

____

____

____

Core:____

____

____

____

PRODUCT CLASSIFICATIONS

Marketers have developed several product classification schemes based on product characteristics in order to develop marketing strategies for individual products.

- **Nondurable goods**—tangible goods that are normally consumed in one or a few uses (e.g., shampoo)

- **Durable goods**—tangible goods that normally survive many uses (e.g., clothing)
- **Services**—activities, benefits, or satisfactions that are offered for sale (e.g., alterations)

Classify your internship organization's product(s) as above.

____

____

____

____

- **Convenience goods**—consumer usually purchases frequently, immediately, and with minimum effort in comparison and buying (e.g., shampoo)
- **Shopping goods**—in process of selection and purchase, customer usually compares on basis of quality, price, and style (e.g., a sweater)
- **Specialty goods**—significant group of buyers is habitually willing to make special purchase effort for goods with unique characteristics and/or brand identification (e.g., Guess jeans)
- **Unsought goods**—customer does not know about goods or knows about them but does not normally think of buying them; may be made aware of the product through advertising (e.g., cemetery plots, insurance, and "Topsy Tail")

Figure 8-1 compares the characteristics of convenience, shopping, and specialty goods.

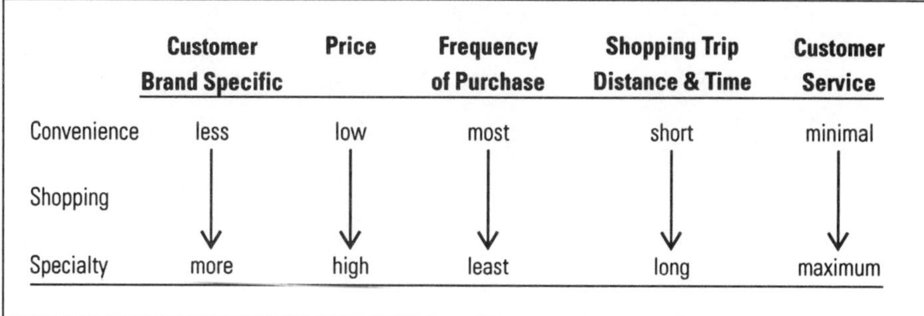

Figure 8-1   *Comparison of convenience, shopping, and specialty goods*

List product classifications (convenience, shopping, and specialty) of your internship operation.

____

____

____

____

____

____

Where is/are the product(s) manufactured? Location of marketing headquarters?

____

____

____

____

____

- **Industrial goods**—are classified in terms of how they enter the production process and their relative costliness. They are separated into three groups:

1. **Materials and parts**—goods that enter the manufacturer's product completely, such as raw materials and manufactured materials and parts

2. **Capital items**—goods that enter the finished product partly, such as installations and accessory equipment
3. **Supplies and services**—items that do not enter the finished product in any form, such as operating supplies and maintenance/repair items, maintenance/repair services, and business advisory services

If your internship organization produces industrial goods, identify the product classifications. If not, provide an example from another company.

- Other product classification terms include:

1. **Fashion goods**—items popular at a specific time
   Staple goods—items constantly in demand and infrequently influenced by fashion changes.
2. **Hard goods**—appliances and home furnishings
   Soft goods—textiles and apparel
3. **High end**—upper price range
   Low end—lower price range
4. **General line**—wide variety of goods
   Limited line—goods within a particular product category

Identify the product classifications of your internship operation according to the terms listed previously.

As the majority of you are working with fashion goods, examine this product classification more closely by discussing fabrications, sizes, and price ranges for a specific line.

BRANDING

The operation often decides whether the firm should put a brand name on its product. Branding can add value to a product and is an important element of the product marketing strategy. Branding terminology includes:

- **Brand:** a name, term, sign, symbol, design, or combination of these that is intended to identify the goods or services of one seller or group of sellers and to differentiate them from those of competitors'
- **Brand name:** the part of a brand that can be vocalized
- **Brand mark:** the part of a brand that can be recognized but cannot be spoken
- **Trademark:** a brand or part of a brand that is given legal protection because it is capable of exclusive rights to use the brand name and/or brand mark
- **Copyright:** the exclusive right to reproduce, publish, and sell the matter in form of a literary, musical, or artistic work

Describe and identify branding usage within your internship organization. If the internship operation does not directly use a brand name, select a product of the inventory for this section.

____

____

____

____

____

____

____

The brand sponsor's decision includes:

- **manufacturer's brand**—also referred to as a national brand
- **private brand**—also called middlemen, distributor, or dealer brand
- **private label**—exclusive to the distributor

What brand sponsor decisions have been implemented by your internship operation?

____

____

____

PACKAGING AND LABELING

Packaging is defined as the activities of designing and producing the container or wrapper for a product. **Labeling** is part of packaging and consists of printed information appearing on or with the package that describes the product. Several factors have contributed to the growth of packaging as an effective marketing tool: convenience, value, consumer affluence, company and brand image, and innovational opportunity.

Discuss the roles of packaging and contributing factors for your internship operation. If the product is a retail operation, packaging would refer to the store exterior and interior facilities, the physical building which contains the core product. Site location should be included in packaging discussion. If your internship operation is a manufacturing firm, describe the types of packaging utilized and the duties of the shipping department's head shipper and packer. Is the product put on hangers, folded, tagged, or boxed individually?

———————————————————————————————

———————————————————————————————

———————————————————————————————

———————————————————————————————

———————————————————————————————

While packaging can refer to the site location and interior/exterior components of the physical plant, the layout of the physical operation is also a consideration. **Layout** refers to planning the internal arrangement of the department with the allocated space of each department. Retailers typically use the following methods for space allocation within the store: industry averages by type of merchandise, sales and productivity of product lines, and model stock. Location of sales-supporting activities are also considered in layout planning.

Sketch the layout of the internship organization's physical plant. Indicate space allocation, merchandise placement (if applicable), department locations, fixturing, lighting, entrances/exits, and traffic flow. In addition, analyze the effectiveness of the layout and, if appropriate, make suggestions for improvement.

Customer Service

In delivering the product to the consumer, the importance of customer relations is significant. Types, levels, and forms of services vary with each type of internship operation. How does the operation handle customer complaints? In addition, how much of the product is offered to the consumer?

To analyze the customer service mix of your organization, answer the following questions in this chapter.

TYPES OF SERVICES

Businesses offer varying levels of service, often reflecting the price ranges of their products. For example, high fashion boutiques carrying expensive designer garments will usually offer a wide range of customer services, from alterations to home delivery. On the other hand, the discount retail operation, such as Sam's Wholesale Club, will provide minimal customer services in an effort to keep prices below those of its competitor's prices. At

Sam's, the customer is not provided with dressing room facilities, packaging, or delivery. The bottom line is that the customer pays for the services offered by the business in two ways: (1) the services are financed through the high markup margins reflected in the retail prices of the products, or (2) the services are sold as entities separate from the products, as in a fee charged for gift wrapping.

What services are included in the customer services mix of your internship organization?

Types of services to consider include:

- delivery reliability
- technical advice
- discounts
- after-sales service
- replacement guarantee
- credit
- delivery service
- alterations
- freight allowances
- ease of payment
- fixture availability
- advertising services
- promotion assistance
- exclusivity arrangements
- courteous and friendly employees
- convenience of location
- ease of contact
- gift wrap
- training of personnel
- lay-away availability
- special order availability

____

____

____

____

____

____

____

____

____

LEVELS OF SERVICE

A business predetermines the amount of service(s) it will provide to its ultimate consumer. The level of service often varies with the type of business. For example, Pay-Less Shoes offers a low level of service while Donegar and Associates resident buying office offers an extremely high (or total) level of customer service.

What level of service is offered in your internship organization? If the internship employer is a manufacturers' representative or apparel producer, how often does she communicate with the retail store buyer and with retail accounts?

FORMS OF SERVICE

Businesses choose to offer their varying levels of services in many forms. One apparel manufacturer may elect to send a merchandise coordinator to a retail outlet to set up displays, train sales personnel, and direct a trunk show. Another manufacturer may prefer to send direct mailers or videotapes featuring new lines to the retail buyer, rather than providing personnel to preview the lines. The identical services can be provided in a multitude of ways. For example, Vanity Fair intimate apparel manufacturers may hire Dupont sales representatives to contact VF retail accounts regarding a national sales promotion for a new fabric innovation.

In what forms are services offered by your internship organization?

____

____

CUSTOMER SERVICE DEPARTMENT

Some business operations have an organized, separate department that has the primary function of servicing the customer. Others divide the customer service responsibilities into several divisions, such as maintenance, credit, and adjustments. Finally, there are organizations that handle the customer service responsibilities informally through management and personnel who have direct contact with the customer.

Customer service department responsibilities include:

1. Customer complaints and adjustments
2. Maintenance service
3. Credit service
4. Technical service
5. Information service

What are the responsibilities of the customer service department within your internship organization? If there is no customer service department, who is responsible for handling this area? Discuss the classifications listed above as they pertain to your internship organization.

____

____

____

____

____

____

____

How are these services (customer complaints and adjustments, technical, credit, information, and maintenance services) coordinated? By whom? Are these services used as tools to create consumer satisfaction and loyalty?

____

____

____

____

____

____

____

THE PRODUCT LINE

A **product line** (or product classification) is a group of products that are closely related, either because they function in a similar manner, are sold to the same customer groups, are marketed through the same types of outlets, or fall within given price ranges. For example, Liz Claiborne produces several product lines; among them, a ladies' sportswear line, a ladies' dress line, a men's wear line, and a fragrance line.

THE PRODUCT MIX

A **product mix** is the set of all product lines and items that a particular seller offers for sale to buyers. It is also referred to as the **product assortment.** For example, Avon's product mix consists of three major product lines: cosmetics, jewelry, and household items. Each product line consists of several sublines. Cosmetics break down into lipstick, nail polish, powder, etc. In total, Avon's product mix includes over 1,300 items.

Product mix dimensions include:

1. **Breadth**—how many different product lines the organization carries

2. **Assortment**—the total number of items in the product mix

3. **Depth**—how many variants are offered in each product of the line
4. **Consistency**—how closely related the various product lines are in end use, production requirements, distribution channels

Categorize your internship organization's product line(s), discussing the assortment and features of each. Within each product line, identify the product mix. Evaluate the breadth, assortment, depth, and consistency of the total product mix.

____

____

____

____

____

____

____

How often does your organization introduce a new product line?

____

____

____

____

____

____

____

____

If your internship employer is a manufacturer or manufacturers' representative, please discuss the product sample line. How frequently is a new sample line prepared? How are seasonal lines categorized? Please compare the depth, breadth, and assortment of these lines. What are the average number of styles and/or units in a sample line? How frequently is the sample line shipped to the manufacturers' rep? Who pays for the sample line? Approximate cost? Are discount terms provided?

____

____

____

____

____

____

____

____

____

____

____

Pricing

Regardless of the organization's product and profit orientation, pricing is central to the decisions that must be made. Something is defined as a product (a good—a dress; a service—a hair cut, or the services offered by an advertising agency; or an idea—the idea that buying union-made products is desirable), and that product is offered to some taker at some price. Normally, we expect that the recipient of the product will pay the price. But, in some cases, the government may completely or partially pay the price. For example, a city or state museum may be open for free some or all of the time because the city or state bears all or part of the burden of covering the costs of its operation. Another illustration is a trade organization, such as the Cotton Council or Wool Bureau, that offers free services of trend forecasting and fabric sourcing to its retail and manufacturing clients. These services are subsidized by the trade organization's members (e.g., cotton and wool producers).

FACTORS IN PRICING DECISIONS

Many factors are taken into account in an organization's pricing decisions. These include costs, the characteristics of the target market(s), the number and characteristics of channel members, the nature of competition, standard trade practices in a particular industry, habit, and legal restrictions.

Legal restrictions have to do with the role of government in the establishment of prices. A primary concern of the government is price-fixing. The Robinson-Patman Act prohibits price discrimination to channel members unless the discrimination can be defended on the basis of savings to the seller. In addition, individual states may have laws prescribing the minimum price for which a product may be sold. And finally, consumer legislation, like the legislation banning "bait and switch" pricing tactics, functions to protect the consuming public and is a further reflection of the government's interest in pricing issues.

Demand is also important in understanding pricing. Demand is elastic when changes in price result in changes in demand (e.g., when prices go up, demand decreases, and vice versa). Competition, too, is related, for if your prices go up but those of your competitor remain stable, customers are likely to move from you to your competitor. If, however, prices for everyone in our industry go up and there is no competitor offering a cheaper price, demand is more likely to remain stable. In addition to these factors, **psychological pricing** (odd vs. even endings on retail prices) is important for organizations to understand when setting prices. Psychological pricing assumes that buyers are more attracted to an odd numbered price ($7.95) than to an even numbered price ($8.00) as the odd number infers a sale or bargain price. **Prestige pricing** assumes that customers infer a relationship between price and quality and will not buy a product if the price is too low. **Customary pricing** assumes that customers expect a certain product to be available at a certain price and that significant deviation in either direction from that customary price will result in decreased demand.

PRICING STRATEGIES

A number of pricing strategies are designed to influence demand.

- **A loss-leader,** for example, is a product offered at an extremely low price, thereby generating no profit and perhaps even a loss just to attract customers or get their attention.
- **Promotional pricing** attempts to keep prices at a minimum (resulting in lower-quality services and physical space) in the belief that there are some customers who always are more attracted to low prices.
- **Price skimming** sets the price for a product higher than normal in an attempt to generate a large sales volume early, before competition has a chance to get in and drive prices down.
- **Penetration pricing** is designed to capture a large mass market by offering the product at a low price.

Generally, pricing strategies are focused on increasing market share by increasing sales, or on increasing profits regardless of changes in sales, or on maintaining market share, (e.g., maintaining your position in relation to the position of your competition).

Usually the set price for a product is expected to do two things: (1) cover all the costs associated with the product and (2) provide some amount of profit. Some business organizations do not conduct cost analyses but rather rely on old, rate methods for arriving at a selling price. **Rate methods** would include a standard initial markup, such as simply doubling the cost of a product to determine the retail price. The objective here is to cover all the costs of production and selling and have something left over for profit. Many retailers, for example, set retail prices by using a **cost-plus pricing** strategy. Doubling the cost price to determine the retail price is an example of this method. Other business organizations use **demand pricing** to determine the retail price. This method assumes that there is some relationship between the selling price of an item and the amount that can be sold. A demand-oriented organization first assesses the demand and then determines whether or not it can afford to incur the costs it will take to meet the demand. When the demand for a product is elastic, the organization must determine whether or not it is better to sell many of something at a lesser price or better to sell fewer of the same thing at a higher price. By using **break-even analysis,** one can determine how much of something will have to be sold at a certain price in order to cover all the costs.

To understand your organization's pricing strategy more thoroughly, answer the following questions.

How do costs influence the price set in your organization? What cost factors are most important to the management of your organization? In other words, which cause them the most worry as prices are affected? What two or three cost variables have the greatest impact on cost? And in what ways in the recent past have efforts been made by your organization to reduce the cost of operation?

____

____

____

____

____

____

____

____

How would you describe the method used to select selling prices by your organization? That is, if you are a retailer, how is the selling price (retail price) to the customer determined? Where and how is the decision made to reduce the retail price? In a museum, what determines if and how an entrance fee will be charged? If there is a museum shop, how are the selling prices determined on the items offered for sale? If you are in a position as a manufacturer's representative, how are the prices on merchandise set? How are discount and dating terms determined that may be offered to retail purchasers? How much independence do individual reps have in making adjustments in the terms of purchase? Finally, if you are working with a designer, to what extent are projected costs important in determining which designs are selected for manufacture? What is the procedure for costing out a garment? How much accuracy is expected and who is responsible for doing so? Examples of garment costing sheets (Figure 10-1A, Figure 10-1B, and Figure 10-1C) follow for your review.

DATE __________ LOT # __________ STYLE # 126

CUSTOMER __________ PATTERN REF.# __________

SEASON __________ BUYER __________

MEDIA __________ SUBDIVISION __________

DESCRIPTION:

SIZE RANGE	1	2	3	4	INT 1	INT 2	INT 3
PETITE							
AVERAGE							
TALL	1.50	.81		.03	.67		
WOMENS							

#1 FABRIC/MILL Springs (skirt,sleeve&collar) $2.10-2.45

STYLE # Crash super soft   WIDTH 59/60"

COLOR Bright royal reactive

COLOR

CONTENT 55 Poly/45 Cotton   F-

#2 FABRIC/MILL Springs (bodice,cuffs) $2.10-2.45

STYLE # Crash super soft   WIDTH 59/60"

COLOR White

CONTENT 55 Poly/45 Cotton   F-

#3 FABRIC/MILL $

STYLE #   WIDTH

COLOR

CONTENT   F-

#4 LINING Block&Brian   STYLE # 40 Denier Tricot

COLOR Bone

CONTENT 100%Nylon   WIDTH 108" $ 1.75   F-

COST 26.75   RETAIL

LABEL:

LABEL TYPE: END FOLD ☐ MITERED ☐ LOOP ☐

LABEL ☐
CORE ☐

SIZE RANGE: __________

SHIP DATE: __________

BUY: __________

ESTIMATE: __________

INITIAL: __________

RATIO: __________

CARE CODE: __________

YARDAGE COMMENTS: __________

LENGTHS: Tall 29" Skirt

OTHER NOTES: __________

#1 INTERFACING Handler		BUTTONS: Tex DTM Fab#1			
# 5100	WIDTH 45"	STYLE #	LIGNE	QTY.	$
COLOR White	$ .62	CP-612	36	3+1	5.95gr
		CP-612	24	6+1	2.00gr
#2 INTERFACING					
#	WIDTH	BUTTONS: Button-Tex DTM white			
COLOR	$	CP-612	24	2++	2.00gr
#3 INTERFACING		CLOSURES: Kaim-silver			
#	WIDTH	STYLE #	SIZE	QTY.	$
COLOR	$	Hook & Bar	1 set		.007ea

ZIPPERS:

TYPE	LENGTH	$

TRIM SOURCE Dennison

Belt Hanger

#08300

5"long $.006ea

TRIM SOURCE

ELASTIC: Imperial

STYLE	WIDTH	QTY.	$
	¼"	24"	.035yd

SHOULDER PADS: Signal

STYLE # 5"X8"X18mm $.0825

Foam pad

BELT LOOPS:

WIDTH: $

BELTS: Charming

STYLE # Self fabric#1

Phone harmers w/3/4"long

$ WIDTH 2" $1.45

BIAS

Figure 10-1A *Garment costing sheets*

JACKET OR BLOUSE		SLACKS — SHORTS — SKIRT	
BASIC PREP. — Bundle		**BASIC PREP. — Bundle**	
		POCKETS - Seam Turn Press T. S.	
COLLAR - Seam Turn Press T. S.			
FACING - Seam Label Serge Press			
ARMHOLE		BAND - Seam Turn Press T. S.	
		SEAM SKIRT - Press Seam	
CUFFS - Seam Turn Press T. S.		SIDE SEAM PANTS	
SLEEVE - Seam Dart Press		INSEAM PANTS	
SET CUFFS - Seam Serge C. St.		CROTCH SEAM	
POCKETS - Seam Turn Press T. S.		PRESS SEAMS	
		SET ZIPPER	
DARTS			
BELT - Seam Turn Press T. S.		SET BAND - Serge T. S.	
		TAPE BOTTOM - Serge St.	
SHOULDER SEAM - Tape Press		BLINDSTITCH	
SIDE SEAM - Tape Press		SNAPS	
TRIM ST.		HOOK AND EYE	
SET COLLAR - Serge Swallow		BUTTON MARK	
SET FACE - Ch. S. Press		BUTTON HOLE	
SET ARM HOLE		BUTTONS	
SET POCKETS			
CLIP - Turn Press Face			
SET SLEEVES			
SET ZIPPER			
BLINDSTITCH HEM		CLIP TURN EXAM.	
BUTTON HOLE - Buttons - Mark		FINAL PRESS HANG.	
TACKS		ASS. BELT TAG BAG	
CLIP TURN EXAM			
FINAL PRESS - HANGER			
FINAL INSPECT. - BUTTON			
ASS. BELT. TAG. BAG.		ETC.	
TOTAL		**TOTAL**	
Date:___________		**TOTAL PRICE**	

FORM NO. 21-100
REV. (9-82)

Figure 10-1B *Garment costing sheets*

DRESS OPERATIONS		DRESS OPERATIONS Con't.	
BASIC PREP. — Bundle		**SKIRT DEPARTMENT**	
		PARTS PRESS	
COLLAR - Seam Turn Press T. S.		SKIRT - Seam Pink Serge	
		SKIRT - Dart Shirr Pleat	
FACING - Seam Label Serge Press			
ARMHOLE		JOIN - Seam Tape Measure	
CUFFS - Seam Turn Press T. S.			
SLEEVES - Seam Press Shirr		SET ZIPPER - With Face	
SET CUFFS - Seam Serge C. St.			
		SERGE BOTTOM	
POCKETS - Seam Turn Press T. S.		TAPE BOTTOM	
		STITCH BOTTOM	
DARTS		BLINDSTITCH SLEEVES	
BELT - Seam Turn Press T. S.			
		BLINDSTITCH HEM BTN.	
		BUTTON HOLE MARK	
SHOULDER SEAM - Press		BUTTON HOLE	
SIDE SEAM - Press		BUTTON MARK	
TRIM STITCH		BUTTONS	
SET YOKE - T. S.			
SET COLLAR - Serge Swallow C. S.		TACKS	
SET ARMHOLE		SNAPS	
SET FACING - Serge Edge St.		HOOK AND EYE	
SET LINING - Serge Edge St.		BELT LOOPS	
SET POCKETS - Edge or T. S.		CLIP - Turn Exam	
SET SLEEVES		FINAL PRESS - HANGER	
		FINAL INSPECT. - BUTTON	
		ASS. BELT. TAG. BAG	
CLIP - Turn Press Fac			
		TOTAL	

Style #: _______________________ Final Price _______________

Figure 10-1B (cont.) *Garment costing sheets*

Samp. Yd.	Dup. Yd.	Stock Yd.	Yd.		Samp. Cost	Dup. Cost	Stock Cost	Cost
				Yds. Self				
				Yds. Comb. I				
				Yds. Comb. II				
				Yds. Comb. III				
				Yds. Comb. IV				
				Yds. Send Out Self				
				Yds. Send Out Comb.				
				Lining I				
				Lining II				
				Fusing Labor				
				Belt				
				Cording				
				Spaghetti				
				Cut Spaghetti				
				Cutting Bias				
				Buckles				
				Yds. Lace				
				Yds. Braid				
				Yds. Ribbons				
				Buttons				
				Buttons				
				Zippers (placket)				
				Other Zippers				
				Snaps, Seam Tape, Thread and Labels				
				Pleating, Shirr				
				Tucking				
				Embroid.				

SWATCH	**MATERIAL**
	FREIGHT
	TOTAL

Figure 10-1C *Garment costing sheets*

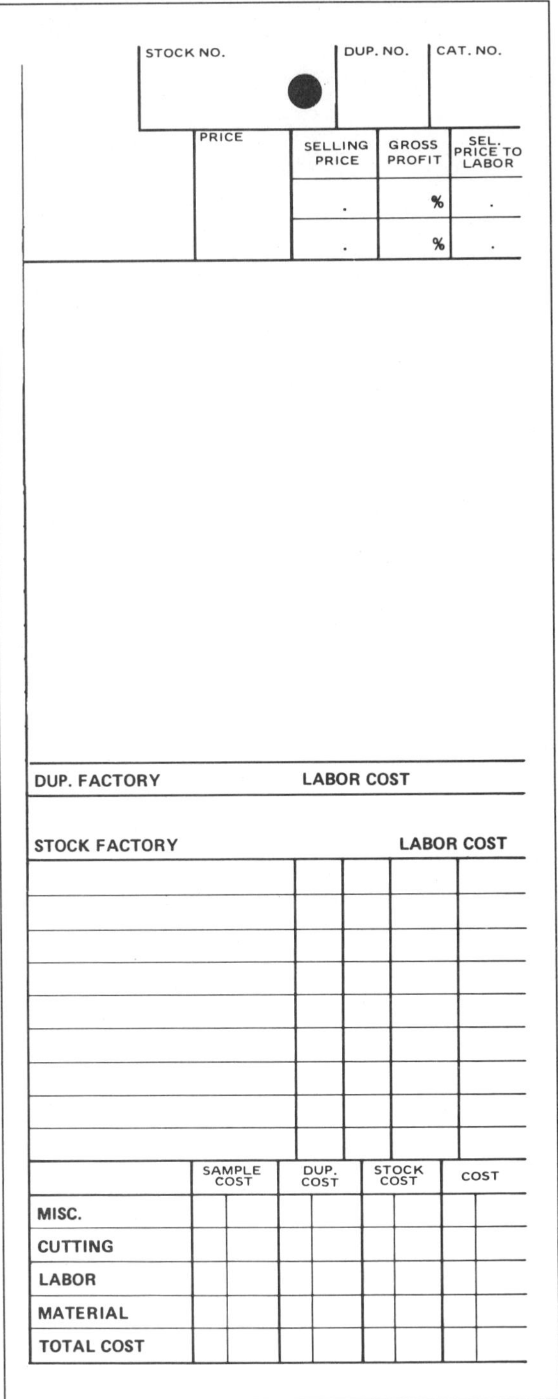

Figure 10-1C (cont.) *Garment costing sheets*

In what ways do government and the law affect the pricing practices of your organization? What law(s) are the most important in the operationalizing of your organization's pricing decisions? How well-informed are decision makers in your organization about the legal restrictions on pricing policies and practices? Where would you go to get legal information on pricing practices if you were in management in your organization? Generally, how much concern is given to the legal implication of pricing practices?

To what extent is psychological pricing important to your organization? Several examples of psychological pricing have been mentioned. Are any of these used and how? Is there concern for the psychological response of consumers to price that you hear informally in your organization, like the timing of marked down merchandise, for example?

Describe price changes (markdowns, reductions) made to move slow-selling or unsold merchandise. If your internship employer is a retailer or manufacturer, how often are price reductions taken? What is the organization's markdown policy? What is the common reduction percent for a given period time? For example, merchandise that has not sold in a thirty-day period may be reduced thirty percent off retail. If your internship employer is a manufacturers' rep, does he have the option to assist retailers with poor selling goods through such alternatives as returns, exchanges, or markdown allowances? See Figure 10-2 for a timing calendar.

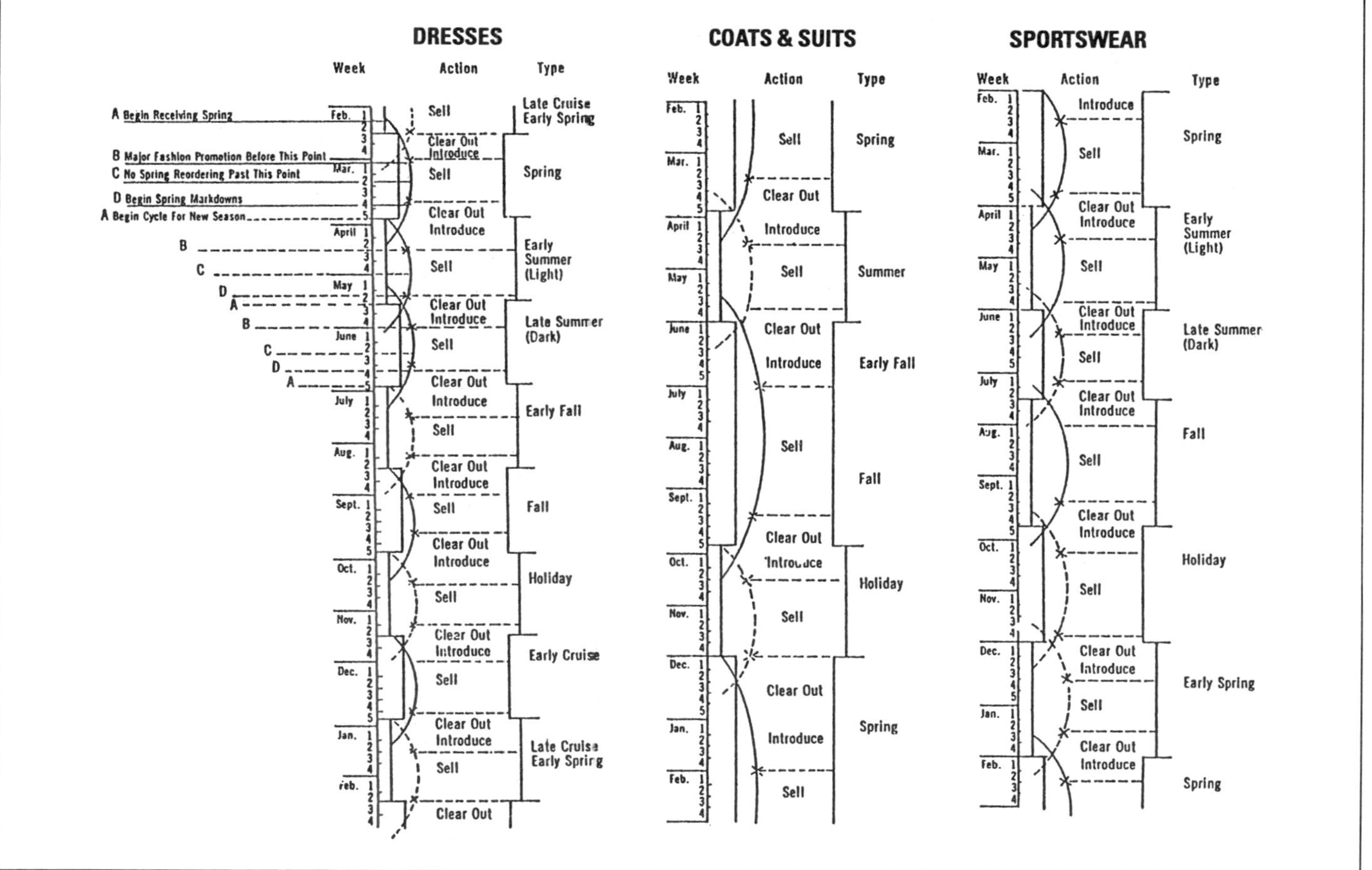

Figure 10-2 *Timing calendar*

How important is habit to the pricing decisions of your organization? That is, to what extent are pricing decisions made a certain way because "that's how we have always done it"? And to what extent is standard trade practice important in pricing decisions? That is, to what extent are things done a certain way because "that's how everybody in this industry does it"? As you look critically at your organization, can you see any decisions regarding pricing that are made out of habit that would be more profitable if made by more critical analysis?

Discuss the accepted merchandising statistics for your internship organization type (e.g., specialty store, apparel manufacturer, or discount outlet) and your merchandise classification (e.g., sportswear, children's wear, or accessories), including stock turnover, initial markup, maintained markup, markdown percent, shortage percent, etc.

Distribution

A **marketing channel** performs the function of moving goods from producers to consumers. Participants in the marketing channel may perform a variety of functions, including research, promotion, contact, matching, negotiation, physical distribution, financing, and risk-taking. Many producers lack the financial resources or interest in carrying out direct marketing, so when some functions are shifted to middlemen, the producer's costs and prices are often lowered. Producers who can afford to establish their own channels can often earn a greater return by increasing their investment in the main business. Efficiency and effectiveness factors should determine marketing channel selections.

CONVENTIONAL MARKETING CHANNELS

A **conventional marketing channel** consists of independent producer(s), wholesaler(s), and retailer(s). Each is a separate business entity, working to maximize its own profits. No channel member has substantial control over the other members.

Examples of conventional marketing channel levels are:

Manufacturer ⟶ Consumer
Manufacturer ⟶ Retailer ⟶ Consumer
Manufacturer ⟶ Wholesaler ⟶ Retailer ⟶ Consumer
Manufacturer ⟶ Wholesaler ⟶ Jobber ⟶ Retailer ⟶ Consumer

Which channels are used by your internship organization to move goods from producers to consumers? Why?

____

____

____

____

____

MARKETING CHANNEL FLOWS

The organizations that compose the marketing channel are connected by physical, title, payment, and information flows. The **physical flow** refers to the movement of the actual product from raw materials to end users. The **title flow** denotes passage of ownership from one marketing organization to another. **Payment flow** describes both the methods channel members use to pay their bills and to whom the payments are made. Finally, the **information flow** pertains to directed promotion efforts used to influence product sales from one party to other parties in the channel.

Describe and evaluate the marketing channel flows within a channel of distribution of your internship organization.

____

____

____

____

____

____

____

____

____

____

____

____

____

VERTICAL MARKETING CHANNELS

A **vertical marketing channel** (or vertical integration) consists of producer(s), wholesaler(s), and retailer(s) cooperating as a unified group. One channel member either owns the others, franchises them, or dominates. There are three types of vertical marketing systems: corporate, contractual, and administered. The **corporate vertical system** combines successive stages of production and distribution under single ownership. A **contractual vertical system** consists of independent firms at different levels of production and distribution integrating their programs on retailer cooperatives and franchise organizations. The **administered vertical marketing system** coordinates successive stages of production and distribution through the size and power of one of the parties, not through common ownership. The new competition in retailing is no longer between independent business units but between vertical marketing systems competing against each other to achieve the best cost economies and customer response.

Is your internship organization using a vertical marketing system? If so, please describe. If not, discuss another organization that utilizes a vertical marketing system.

____

____

____

____

____

____

What are the strengths and limitations of the vertical marketing system?

____

____

____

____

HORIZONTAL AND MULTICHANNEL MARKETING CHANNELS

The **horizontal marketing channel** is the joining of two or more companies to take advantage of an emerging marketing channel opportunity by contracting on a permanent or temporary basis or by creating a separate company. **Multichannel marketing systems** operate on two different customer levels (**dual distribution**). They usually combine several styles of retailing with an integrating of some distribution and management functions. For example, Esprit markets its product line directly to the consumer through its retail outlets yet also sells its product line to other retail stores that market the products to the consumer.

Does your internship organization use a horizontal or multichannel marketing system? Please explain.

____

____

____

____

____

____

What are the advantages and disadvantages of these systems?

____

____

____

CHANNEL DESIGN ALTERNATIVES

The company sales force, a manufacturer's promotional agency, and industrial distributors are examples of business intermediaries that are considered when determining channel design. Sometimes a company attempts to develop a preferred channel but ventures into another channel due to cost or difficulty factors. For example, the U.S. Timex Company originally tried to sell its inexpensive Timex watches to fine jewelry stores. However, as most jewelry stores refused to purchase the low-end watches, Timex turned to mass-merchandise outlets. The choice was advantageous due to the future rapid growth of mass-merchandising.

Distribution strategies include an intensive, exclusive, or selective number of intermediaries. Hanes Hosiery utilizes an **intensive distribution** strategy, selling its products to discount and moderate-priced retailers throughout the country. The company's goal is to make its product line available to as many different types of retail operations as possible—the objective of intensive distribution. Liz Claiborne uses a **selective distribution** strategy, choosing to sell its lines to moderate and better department and specialty stores. Escada, a German sportswear firm, has chosen an **exclusive distribution** strategy, selecting preferred better stores due to the company's high-end price points and limited production capacity. In this case, an exclusive distribution strategy satisfies Escada's desire to make its high quality, limited product available to a specific high-end clientele. Cost, control, and length of commitment should be evaluated when formulating the channel design.

Discuss the channel design used by your internship organization.

CHANNEL MANAGEMENT

In order to effectively implement and manage the channel design, channel participants must be carefully selected, motivated, and evaluated. The producer will want to analyze the location of middlemen, future growth potential, and type of clientele. Motivation techniques include cooperation (higher margins, cooperative advertising), partnership, or distribution programming (a marketing department to identify distributors' needs). The producer must periodically evaluate the performance of middlemen against such standards as sales quota attainment, average inventory levels, delivery times, cooperation, and handling of defective or lost merchandise.

How does your internship organization select and motivate channel members?

Describe evaluation methods used by your internship organization to identify effective and ineffective middlemen.

____

____

____

____

PHYSICAL DISTRIBUTION

Physical distribution involves the tasks of planning, implementing, and controlling the physical flows of materials and final goods from points of origin to points of use to meet the needs of customers at a profit. The objective of physical distribution is getting the right goods to the right places at the right times for the least cost. The major physical distribution cost is transportation, followed by warehousing, inventory carrying, receiving and shipping, packaging, administration, and order processing. In summary, physical distribution describes how companies store, handle, and move goods so they will be available to the consumer at the right time and location.

Analyze physical distribution methods of your internship organization by answering the following questions.

*How are the orders handled (**order processing**)? By whom? Are reorders handled differently?*

____

____

____

____

____

*Where are the stocks located (**warehousing**)?*

____

____

____

____

____

____

*How much stock is kept on hand (**inventory**)?*

____

____

____

____

____

____

*How are goods shipped (**transportation**)?*

____

____

____

____

____

____

*How quickly does the producer ship the product to the consumer? What is the time period between order receipt by the producer and the receipt of goods by the consumer (**lead time**)?*

____

____

____

____

____

____

Promotion

Promotion communicates the product attributes to the target consumers through four major tools: **advertising, sales promotion,** publicity, and **personal selling.** Promotion decisions include: 1. identifying the target market, 2. choosing a message (personal vs. nonpersonal), 3. choosing the media, 4. setting the total promotion budget and mix, and 5. collecting feedback. In this chapter, you will examine the promotion decisions as they relate to the promotion mix tools and your internship operation.

IDENTIFYING THE TARGET MARKET

The preliminary stage of promotion decision making includes identifying the **target market** and determining the **buyer readiness state** to achieve the desired audience response. Promotional efforts can address the consumer on cognitive, affective, or behavioral levels. A promotion for a new product often focuses on the consumer's **cognitive state**—awareness and knowledge—in order to introduce the product to the consumer. Promotions of existing products often appeal to the consumer's **affective state**—feelings, preferences, and convictions. Promotions that attempt to motivate the consumer to purchase the product immediately—like K-Mart's "blue light specials"—appeal to the consumer's **behavioral state**—his tendency to act spontaneously.

Examine and identify 1. your internship operation's target market and 2. its buyer readiness state.

____

____

____

____

____

CHOOSING A MESSAGE

The second promotion decision works toward developing an effective message that generates attention, stimulates an interest, promotes a desire, and induces action. The message can be segmented into three parts: **content, structure,** and **format.** The message content reaches out to the target market through a rational, emotional, or moral appeal. The **rational appeal** stresses self-interest by showing that the product will produce claimed benefits. The positive or negative **emotional appeal** may be based on fear, love, humor, pride, romance, or joy. **Moral appeals** reflect the audience's sense of what is right or wrong. The message structure may be open-ended or closed; one- or two-sided; or present the strongest argument first or last. The message format varies with the type of media. Size, color, and illustration are all parts of print or display media messages. The speech pace and background music of a radio message are segments of the message format.

Select a promotional effort of your internship operation and analyze its message purpose, appeal, content, structure, and format.

____

____

____

____

____

____

____

____

____

____

PERSONAL VERSUS NONPERSONAL COMMUNICATION CHANNELS

In the third stage of the promotion decision process, personal or nonpersonal communication channels are selected. **Personal communication channels** are classified as advocate, expert, or social channels. The **advocate channel** uses salespersons to contact potential buyers in the target market. The **expert channel** uses an individual person with expertise to make statements to the target market. Word-of-mouth from neighbors, family, friends, and associates composes the **social channel.** Personal communication channels are stimulated by identifying influential individuals and organizations; creating opinion leaders; working through community influentials; and developing advertising with high conversation value.

Nonpersonal communication channels utilize **mass media** (undifferentiated) or **selective** (specialized) **media** through print, electronic, or display methods. Nonpersonal communication channels also include atmospheres—designed environments that create or reinforce the buyer's product desire. For example, Esprit sportswear manufacturing company decorates its California showroom with antique Amish quilts, lush green plants, and natural wood furniture. The contemporary decor creates an exciting and colorful atmosphere that reflects Esprit's product line.

Events, as nonpersonal communication channels, are designed occurrences that communicate particular messages to the target audience. The Milliken Breakfast Show, sponsored by the textile manufacturer, is a stage presentation designed to familiarize retail buyers with innovative fabrications introduced by the company. Neiman Marcus' Fortnight presentations communicate messages to the target market using a particular country as the theme.

Examine the personal communication channels used by your internship organization. Are they advocate, expert, and/or social channels? How does the organization stimulate personal communication channels?

____

____

____

____

____

____

____

Identify the nonpersonal communication channels of your internship organization. Do they utilize mass or selective media? How are atmospheres or events used as nonpersonal communication channels?

____

____

____

____

____

____

____

CHOOSING THE MEDIA TYPE

The **reach** (number of persons in the target market), **frequency** (number of times the message is presented), and **impact** of the media source are examined when choosing the media type. Variables to consider include target market media habits, the product itself, the message, and the cost. **Source credibility** is also examined for the purposes of establishing expertise, trustworthiness, and likability. For example, J.C. Penney uses the media of television to visually present the Jacqueline Ferrar collection on glamorous, active women.

Select a promotion effort of your internship operation and identify its media source and featured product. Analyze the target market media habits, message, and cost as these variables relate to the product. Examine the source credibility, media reach, frequency, and impact of the media source.

SETTING THE PROMOTION BUDGET

Methods for establishing an organization's total **promotion budget** vary within different industries. Revlon cosmetic firm allocates 7% of sales volume for promotion expenditures while K-Mart appropriates 2.2% of sales volume for promotion costs. Four techniques are used to set the total promotion budget of an organization:

- the **affordable method,** the dollar amount the firm can afford at the moment;
- the **percentage of sales method,** as based on sales volume;
- the **competitive-parity method,** based on competitor's expenditures; and
- the **analysis and costing of communication objectives and tasks.**

Promotion budget assistance is often provided by external funding. Fiber, fabric, and garment producers frequently offer **cooperative advertising** monies. In exchange for name or brand recognition, the producer will pay a specified percentage of promotion costs. The Wool Bureau and the Cotton Council provide cooperative advertising funds to garment manufacturers and retailers promoting their respective fabrics.

Which method is used by your internship organization? Why is this method preferred? Is external funding utilized? If so, what are the sources? If not, are such funds available? Where?

____

____

____

____

____

____

SETTING THE PROMOTION MIX

Once the promotion budget is determined, it is divided between the four promotion tools: advertising, sales promotion, personal selling, and publicity.

Advertising is the use of paid media to communicate persuasive information about the product in a nonpersonal presentation financed by the seller. Advertising media forms include magazines and newspapers, television and radio, outdoor displays, direct mail, novelties (e.g., calendars, memo tablets), automotive placards, catalogs, directories, and circulars. Advertising can be designed to serve several purposes. **Institutional advertising** builds the organization image and creates community goodwill. **Brand advertising** promotes a particular brand, while **sale advertising** announces specific value item(s).

Classified advertising spreads information about a sale, service, or event. **Advocacy advertising** supports a particular cause. For example, a retailer recently ran a newspaper advertisement announcing that his entire inventory was composed of American-made products. In the advocacy advertisement, he expressed his personal reasons for supporting domestic producers.

Personal selling consists of oral presentations to one or more prospective buyers for the purpose of making sales. A manufacturer's representative is employed for the purpose of personal selling. Currently, electronic forms of personal selling are rapidly developing through video recording and television.

Sales promotion includes short-term incentives that encourage the product sale. Examples of sales promotion techniques include samples, coupons, price packs, point-of-purchase displays, trade promotions, contests, sweepstakes, games, business conventions, and trade shows. An externally-sponsored sales promotion example is the Chic Jeans giveaway. The consumer purchased a pair of Chic Jeans and then received a free jacket by submitting the sales receipt, coupon, and label to the manufacturer. The promotion was of no cost to the retailer, as all expenses were incurred by Chic.

Publicity refers to the nonpersonal creation of demand for a product by introducing commercially significant news about the product through media efforts not paid by the sponsor. Press relations, product publicity, corporate communication, lobbying, and counseling are examples of publicity efforts. As an example, Jones Store Company, a Kansas City department store, recruited designer Bill Blass to promote his fashions and fragrances within the store. The *Kansas City Star* newspaper featured several articles on the designer's background, current lines, interests, and activities while mentioning his appearance at Jones Store Company. The retailer paid nothing for the newspaper recognition.

Examine the advertising efforts of your internship organization. Choose several advertising samples and describe the purpose and media type of each ad. List all forms of advertising media utilized by your organization.

Are your internship organization's advertising efforts externally or internally sponsored, or a combination of both? If your internship organization does minimal advertising, locate advertising examples from other sources to illustrate your understanding of advertising concepts.

Does your internship organization utilize promotional assistance provided by suppliers? Special events, personnel training programs, trunk shows, giveaways, purchase with purchase items, catalogues, brochures, and direct mailers are some of the promotional alternatives offered by some vendors (e.g., fiber or apparel manufacturers). Describe promotional assistance used by your internship organization.

Describe the personal selling efforts of your internship organization. How many people are responsible for personal selling? Diagram the organizational structures of its personal selling staff, if applicable.

Have personal selling strategies changed over the past few years? Analyze current and future personal selling transitions.

Describe sales promotion efforts within your internship organization. Are they internally or externally sponsored? If your organization offers no sales promotion activities, locate an example from another source.

____

____

____

____

____

____

____

Analyze the publicity efforts of your internship organization. Locate examples of both positive and negative publicity illustrations. What techniques are used by your organization to gain positive publicity? If publicity solicitation is not applied, what suggestions can you offer to gain favorable publicity for your organization?

____

____

____

____

____

____

____

____

VISUAL MERCHANDISING

Displays are often called "silent salespersons." They communicate information to the consumer, affecting purchasing behavior. Effective use of visual merchandising can modify consumer demand, buying habits, and patronage. Creative use of space creates expectations through stimulation. The primary purpose of a display is to sell product(s) while projecting a correct image. Displays can also speed up transactions, as in a self-service operation. Window and interior displays are classified as institutional, point-of-purchase, seasonal, open, closed, or atmosphere.

Analyze the use of displays for creating sales within your internship organization, or locate an example elsewhere.

____

____

____

____

____

____

____

____

____

COLLECTING FEEDBACK

Evaluating the results of promotion efforts is a crucial, yet often overlooked, stage of promotion decision-making. The most common form of promotion evaluation is an analysis of sales and profit impact before, during, and after the promotion effort occurs. Consumer surveys are sometimes used to evaluate consumer awareness, comprehension, and attitude changes resulting from promotion efforts. Advertising pretesting includes **direct ratings** (which ad would influence you to buy the product?) and **portfolio tests,** in which a group of consumers analyzes an assortment of ads and then is tested for recall and recognition.

Which evaluation methods are used by your internship organization to evaluate promotion results? Which methods would you recommend? What are the disadvantages to the traditional technique of measuring sales and profit impact before, during, and after the occurrence of a promotion effort?

 *ppendix A*

Employer/Student/Academic Sponsor Agreement for the Internship

Please type all responses except signatures. All 3 parties (the employer, student and academic sponsor) should retain a copy of this agreement.

Employer (name of organization): _______________________________

Address: ____

____

Job description (List the duties, goals, and responsibilities that the internship student will have. If possible, the duties and goals should be listed in an internship calendar format.):

____

____

____

____

Time commitment (number of weeks, days per week, hours per day):

____

Amount of academic credit to be earned for internship course:

____

Level of academic credit to be earned for internship course:

____

Approvals

1. Approval of internship employer. I agree to supervise this student, to expose this student to information sources needed to complete *A Guide to Analyzing Your Fashion Industry Internship,* and to evaluate this student's work performance.

   Name ____

   Title ____

   Signature ____

   Telephone ____

2. Approval of academic internship sponsor. I approve the placement as described.

   Name____

   Signature ____

   Academic Institution ____

   Telephone ____

3. Approval of student. I agree to complete *A Guide to Analyzing Your Fashion Industry Internship* and to provide my employer with high quality work performance.

   Name ________________ Year in school ________________

   Signature ________________ Student number ________________

   Address during internship: ________________

   ____

   Telephone number ____
   (area code)

 ppendix B

WEEKLY ACTIVITY REPORT FORMS

Introduction to Weekly Activity Report Forms

The *Weekly Activity Reports* that follow are similar to a reflection paper or a weekly journal. It is suggested that during your internship you maintain a small notebook in which you can jot down information you will need to remember, things to do, and brief summaries of your daily activities. From this working notebook, you can construct an effective *Weekly Activity Report*.

An effective *Weekly Activity Report:*

1. Contains entries that indicate dates, hours worked, a description of job responsibilities for each day, and reflections of your work week.
2. May include a few brief entries, while others may be several pages in length.
3. Indicates what you have learned from each work week. Sometimes you learn what not to do, what you should have done, how to handle problems, etc.
4. Is drafted daily. If you attempt to reconstruct a week's worth of work, it will be obvious.
5. Concludes with a final entry that summarizes your views of the internship experience.

An ineffective *Weekly Activity Report:*

1. Is sloppy, too brief, vague, and boring to review. It is more like a log of work hours than a reflection and evaluation of your weekly work experiences.

2. Contains entries that are not written weekly with little attention to detail.

3. Often says, "same as yesterday." Most employees learn something new each day (we hope!), although some days the learning is more subtle. An ineffective *Weekly Activity Report* looks just at the surface, rather than inward.

WEEKLY ACTIVITY REPORT FORM

Student intern's name ________________________________ Week number ______

Date _________________ Company name ________________________________

Work schedule

Date	Day of week	From	To	# of hours worked	Primary duties
	M				
	Tu				
	W				
	Th				
	F				
	Sa				
	Su				

Total hours worked this week ______

Descriptive summary of this week's activities (include duties performed, training, exposures to new areas of the business organization, etc.):

____

____

____

____

____

____

____

WEEKLY ACTIVITY REPORT FORM (continued)

Positive learning experiences: _______________________________________

____

____

____

____

____

Negative learning experiences: _______________________________________

____

____

____

____

____

Self-evaluation of this week's performance: ______________________________

____

____

____

____

Signature of student _______________________________________

Signature of internship employer _______________________________

WEEKLY ACTIVITY REPORT FORM

Student intern's name _________________________________ Week number ______

Date _________________ Company name _______________________________

Work schedule

Date	Day of week	From	To	# of hours worked	Primary duties
	M				
	Tu				
	W				
	Th				
	F				
	Sa				
	Su				

Total hours worked this week ______

Descriptive summary of this week's activities (include duties performed, training, exposures to new areas of the business organization, etc.):

____

____

____

____

____

____

____

____

WEEKLY ACTIVITY REPORT FORM (continued)

Positive learning experiences: _______________________________________

____

____

____

____

____

____

Negative learning experiences: _______________________________________

____

____

____

____

____

Self-evaluation of this week's performance: __________________________

____

____

____

____

Signature of student _____________________________________

Signature of internship employer _________________________

WEEKLY ACTIVITY REPORT FORM

Student intern's name _______________________________ Week number ______

Date ___________ Company name _______________________________

Work schedule

Date	Day of week	From	To	# of hours worked	Primary duties
	M				
	Tu				
	W				
	Th				
	F				
	Sa				
	Su				

Total hours worked this week ______

Descriptive summary of this week's activities (include duties performed, training, exposures to new areas of the business organization, etc.):

____

____

____

____

____

____

____

WEEKLY ACTIVITY REPORT FORM (continued)

Positive learning experiences: ______________________________________

____

____

____

____

____

____

Negative learning experiences: ______________________________________

____

____

____

____

____

Self-evaluation of this week's performance: ______________________________

____

____

____

____

____

Signature of student ____

Signature of internship employer _________________________________

WEEKLY ACTIVITY REPORT FORM

Student intern's name _______________________________ Week number _________

Date _________ Company name _______________________________________

Work schedule

Date	Day of week	From	To	# of hours worked	Primary duties
	M				
	Tu				
	W				
	Th				
	F				
	Sa				
	Su				

Total hours worked this week _______

Descriptive summary of this week's activities (include duties performed, training, exposures to new areas of the business organization, etc.):

____

____

____

____

____

____

____

____

WEEKLY ACTIVITY REPORT FORM (continued)

Positive learning experiences: _______________________________________

____

____

____

____

____

____

Negative learning experiences: _______________________________________

____

____

____

____

____

Self-evaluation of this week's performance: _______________________________

____

____

____

____

Signature of student ____

Signature of internship employer _______________________________________

WEEKLY ACTIVITY REPORT FORM

Student intern's name _______________________________ Week number _________

Date _________ Company name _______________________________

Work schedule

Date	Day of week	From	To	# of hours worked	Primary duties
	M				
	Tu				
	W				
	Th				
	F				
	Sa				
	Su				

Total hours worked this week ______

Descriptive summary of this week's activities (include duties performed, training, exposures to new areas of the business organization, etc.):

____

____

____

____

____

____

____

____

WEEKLY ACTIVITY REPORT FORM (continued)

Positive learning experiences: _______________________________________

____

____

____

____

____

____

Negative learning experiences: _______________________________________

____

____

____

____

____

Self-evaluation of this week's performance: _____________________________

____

____

____

____

Signature of student _______________________________________

Signature of internship employer _______________________________

WEEKLY ACTIVITY REPORT FORM

Student intern's name _______________________________ Week number _________

Date _________ Company name _______________________________

Work schedule

Date	Day of week	From	To	# of hours worked	Primary duties
	M				
	Tu				
	W				
	Th				
	F				
	Sa				
	Su				

Total hours worked this week _______

Descriptive summary of this week's activities (include duties performed, training, exposures to new areas of the business organization, etc.):

____

____

____

____

____

____

____

WEEKLY ACTIVITY REPORT FORM (continued)

Positive learning experiences: _______________________________________

____

____

____

____

____

____

Negative learning experiences: _______________________________________

____

____

____

____

____

Self-evaluation of this week's performance: _______________________________

____

____

____

____

Signature of student _______________________________________

Signature of internship employer _______________________________

SUMMARY OF INTERNSHIP WEEKLY ACTIVITY

List the weekly routine duties of the ________________________________.

(internship employer's job title)

____

____

____

____

____

List your weekly routine duties as the student intern.

____

____

____

____

____

As in most industries, various segments of the fashion industry have unique "buzz words"—terminology (phrases or words) used by industry personnel. List these terms and the appropriate definitions.

____

____

____

____

____

____

SUMMARY OF INTERNSHIP WEEKLY ACTIVITY
(continued)

Indicate your income (internship salary), if your internship was paid, and any expenses you incurred during your internship experience.

____

____

____

Indicate the anticipated salary range for a career in _______________________ .
(employer's position)

From your internship experience, examine the qualifications and attributes of a successful _____________________.
(employer's position)

____

____

____

____

From your experience, examine the qualifications and attributes of a successful student intern in this type of internship position.

____

____

____

____

Which areas of study would assist a student preparing for a career in this employment area?

____

____

Appendix C

EVALUATION FORMS

Evaluation of the Internship Organization

Please rate the product success requirements and marketing activities to reflect your perceptions of the internship organization:

Product Success Requirements—Rating

	Highest			Lowest	
	5	4	3	2	1
1. Company personality and good will					
2. Marketing					
3. Research and development					
4. Personnel					
5. Finance					
6. Production					
7. Location and facilities					
8. Purchasing and supplies					

Marketing Activities—Rating

		Highest			Lowest	
		5	4	3	2	1
1.	Pricing	1.				
2.	Customer services	2.				
3.	Sales personnel management	3.				
4.	Product research and development	4.				
5.	Marketing cost budgeting and control	5.				
6.	Physical distribution	6.				
7.	Market research	7.				
8.	Marketing organization structure	8.				
9.	Advertising and sales promotion planning	9.				
10.	Distribution channel control	10.				
11.	Extending customer credit	11.				
12.	Public relations	12.				

Evaluation of Student Intern by Employer

Date of evaluation ______________________

Student's name ____

Job title/dept. ____

Semester/term of internship ____________________________________

Organization's name and address ________________________________

____

____

Supervisor's name and title ____________________________________

____

Telephone number ____

Brief description of student intern's job responsibilities:

____

____

____

____

Please rank the following characteristics of the student employee.

	Highest Performance				Lowest Performance
1. Motivation	5	4	3	2	1
2. Attitude	5	4	3	2	1
3. Ability	5	4	3	2	1
4. Appearance	5	4	3	2	1
5. Organization	5	4	3	2	1
6. Self-direction	5	4	3	2	1
7. Attendance/punctuality	5	4	3	2	1
8. Interpersonal skills	5	4	3	2	1
9. Leadership ability	5	4	3	2	1

Evaluation of Student Intern by Employer (*continued*)

Did the student complete the training program for the internship effectively and within the allocated time? ________ Yes ________ No

Additional comments/recommendations:

____

____

____

____

____

____

____

____

Are you interested in sponsoring a student intern again in the future?
______ Yes ______ No

If so, please list contact person, phone number, and location for each job opportunity.

____

____

____

____

____

Is it acceptable to forward a copy of this evaluation to the student intern?
______ Yes ______ No

On a grading scale of A through F, what grade would you assign to the student intern? ____________________

Signature ____

Student Evaluation of Employer

Evaluation date _______________________

Student name _______________________________________

Title/dept. _______________________________________

Semester/term of internship _______________________________

Organization name and address ____________________________

____

____

____

Supervisor's name and title _______________________________

____

Telephone number _______________________________________

Please give a brief description of your job responsibilities:

____

____

____

____

____

____

Student Evaluation of Employer (continued)

Please rate the following characteristics of the employer:

	Highest Performance				Lowest Performance
1. Assistance/training	5	4	3	2	1
2. Attitude	5	4	3	2	1
3. Support	5	4	3	2	1
4. Direction/goal setting	5	4	3	2	1
5. Communications	5	4	3	2	1
6. Overall supervision	5	4	3	2	1

Additional comments/recommendations:

____

____

____

____

____

____

____

____

____

____

Would you recommend this organization to future internship candidates?

_______ Yes _______ No

If so, please list contact person, location, and telephone number.

____

____

____

Signature ____

Self-Evaluation by Student Intern

Date of evaluation ___________________

Your name ___________________________________

Job title/dept. _______________________________

Semester/term of internship ____________________

Organization's name and address _______________

____

____

Supervisor's name and title ____________________

____

Telephone number ____________________________

Brief description of your internship job responsibilities:

____

____

____

____

Please rank yourself on the following characteristics as they reflect your performance during the internship experience:

	Highest Performance				Lowest Performance
1. Motivation	5	4	3	2	1
2. Attitude	5	4	3	2	1
3. Ability	5	4	3	2	1
4. Appearance	5	4	3	2	1
5. Organization	5	4	3	2	1
6. Self-direction	5	4	3	2	1
7. Attendance/punctuality	5	4	3	2	1
8. Interpersonal skills	5	4	3	2	1
9. Leadership ability	5	4	3	2	1

Did you complete the training program for the internship effectively and within the allocated time? _______ Yes _______ No

Additional comments/recommendations:

____

____

____

____

____

____

____

____

Are you interested in working as a student intern again in the future?
_______ Yes _______ No _______ Not applicable

On a grading scale of A through F, what grade would you assign to yourself as a student intern? _______________________

Signature ____

Appendix D

CAREER OPTIONS IN THE FASHION INDUSTRY

If you love fashion, you are certainly not alone. Last year, consumers spent more than $120 billion on apparel. Is it possible to transfer a fascination for clothes into a challenging and rewarding career? The answer is an enthusiastic "yes!" Current employment statistics provide insight into the opportunities available in the fashion industry. One out of every eight workers in the United States is employed by the apparel industry or one of its allied fields. Textile and clothing manufacturers represent the largest employer of women and minorities, with more than two million workers. There are some 5,500 apparel producers in New York City alone and more than 110,000 U.S. retailers specializing in clothing and accessories. Another 70,000 retailers carry fashion goods as classifications within their merchandise assortments.

Employment opportunities within the industry have never been more diverse. Career options range from the artistic to the scientific, from the creative to the quantitative, and from manufacturing to retailing. In addition to the traditional careers in design, buying, and sales, there are numerous positions being created in such areas as visual merchandising, product development, computer-aided design, wardrobe consultation, merchandise coordination, and fashion journalism.

The majority of these career tracks are prefaced with college studies in fashion merchandising or fashion design. Most retailers and manufacturers consider the bachelor's degree a prerequisite for employment and many prefer a liberal arts program, due to its broad and integrated approach to education. Success at any level of the fashion industry seems to demand an overall understanding of the various factors influencing the business at any given point in time. Most of the industry leaders are characterized by high energy levels, dedication to their work, and an insatiable desire for knowledge and information.

A typical degree program in fashion merchandising incorporates studies of textiles, design principles, product analysis, management, advertising, marketing, managerial accounting, and computer science. Fashion design curriculums generally focus on history of dress, clothing construction, pattern making, draping, drawing, and textile analysis. College graduates can expect salaries of $18,000 to $28,000 for most entry-level positions in fashion manufacturing and retailing. The business is fast paced and results oriented, so advancement opportunities abound for individuals committed to their careers.

There is little doubt that fashion industry employers prefer job candidates with previous exposure to the business. Consequently, college graduates with prior experience in retailing or manufacturing have an edge over the competition when interviewing for entry-level positions. To gain work experience while in college, students may elect to check the classified section of their local newspapers. It will generally list openings for receptionists, receiving assistants, and sales clerks. In addition, many apparel manufacturers take on temporary help during peak shipping seasons. For upper-level students, the internship provides an in-depth work experience.

The fashion industry includes the total system of business activities designed to develop, market, and distribute apparel and accessories. This system is frequently classified according to four levels of operation: primary producers, secondary producers, retailers, and ancillary services.

Primary producers range from Fortune 500 corporations like Du Pont, a major synthetic fiber company, to Southern cotton farms. Textile manufacturers take the raw fiber, whether synthetic or natural, spin it into yarn, and weave or knit it into fabric. Color dyeing and the development of fabric textures, prints, and patterns are included in this level of operation and comprise the principle responsibilities of the textiles designer.

Secondary producers (apparel manufacturers) design, produce, and market clothing to retailers. As unglamourous as it may sound, Ralph Lauren is a manufacturer. Most companies develop five new "lines" a year for presentation to store buyers at the New York and regional apparel markets. A line is a seasonal collection of new merchandise, designed to elicit excitement and orders from retail buyers. This is one of the most creative and emotional levels of the fashion industry where an "up-and-coming" designer can begin and sometimes end a career in just one season. Basically, there are four types of designers: the high fashion or couture designer, the moderate-priced designer, the stylist, and the freelance designer. The couture designer creates custom-made original garments for individual clients and is one of the favored topics of fashion journalists and photographers. The company or moderate designer works for a large, brand-like manufacturer and produces popular-priced fashions with mass appeal. Moderate or budget-priced apparel companies as well as retailers involved in private label product development often use a stylist to adapt or modify styles already proven at retail. Finally, the freelance designer functions as an independent artist, selling new designs and ideas to apparel manufacturers.

Designer positions are few and far between, but for the individuals who have the talent and perseverance to master this career track, the rewards can be great. Adaptability is probably one of the more essential qualities. Many successful designers began their careers as showroom receptionists, sales representatives, sample hands, and assistant pattern makers, then worked their way up through the ranks. Sample hands work closely with designers and are responsible for the construction of sample garments. Pattern makers then "grade" the new designs into sized patterns for manufacturing. Sales representatives present the finished lines to retail buyers across the country and function as intermediaries between the manufacturing and retail sectors.

Retailers, the third industry classification, come in all sizes and shapes. Whether they are catalogue merchants, factory outlets, department stores, specialty stores, or discount stores, they all have one goal in mind—a profitable bottom line. One of the most popular retailing careers is that of the fashion buyer. In general, buyers preview new lines in New York or other regional apparel markets and place orders according to a seasonal plan and budget. There are approximately 40,000 buyers in the U. S. today earning anywhere from $28,000 to $80,000, depending on experience and responsibility. Daily activities include supervision of sales staff, advertising and promotion considerations, negotiations with vendors, and quantitative reviews of merchandise sales, stock levels, and receipt plans. Some senior buyers control retail budgets in excess of $30 million. Advancement opportunities include the supervisory positions of divisional merchandise manager and general merchandise manager. Both of these career options involve increased store management responsibility and income. It is not uncommon for the general merchandise manager of a major retail operation to command a salary of $100,000 or more.

One of the more recent and expanding career options within retailing is that of visual merchandiser. Retail fashion merchandising is more competitive than ever before and often how a store is managed and presented to the public influences sales volume more than the merchandise carried. Visual merchandising is concerned with the development of an aesthetic retail environment, designed to maximize sales. Store displays, signs, fixturing, and merchandise presentation are just some of the responsibilities associated with this highly creative position.

Another new career track in the fashion industry is the merchandise coordinator, a position that bridges the gap between the producer and the retailer. Employed by an apparel or accessories manufacturer, the merchandise coordinator travels to the major retail stores selling the manufacturer's product. At the store, the merchandise coordinator updates displays of the product line, educates the retailer's sales staff, fills in stock gaps, and works directly with the consumers during special promotions. Companies such as Levi, Fossil, and Hot Sox have derived tremendous retail success through the employment of merchandise coordinators.

The final classification, *ancillary services,* includes all the non-retailing or non-manufacturing businesses involved in the fashion industry. Here again, creative and exciting career opportunities abound. Employment options include diverse occupations in fashion advertising, public relations, fashion show production, trend forecasting, marketing, journalism, photography, modeling, illustration, and buying. Resident buyers function as brokers by placing large-scale orders and help clarify fashion trends for member stores. Fashion industry advertising, photography, and modeling agencies help shape these trends. Fashion journalists also play a major role in the analysis of fashion trends. Some of the more notable examples of independent agencies are the Ford Modeling Agency, publications such as *Vogue* and *Women's Wear Daily,* and trend forecasting services such as T.F.S. and Promostyl.

Whatever your area of interest, creative or quantitative, the fashion industry offers a career alternative to suit your aptitudes and skills. The name of the game is to build a career on a subject that you love. Spending forty hours or more per week in an area that you truly enjoy blurs the lines between work, hobby, and relaxation. If fashion is your passion, there are many career options for you to pursue.

Glossary

administered vertical marketing system a marketing channel that co-ordinates successive stages of production and distribution through the size and power of one of the parties, not through common ownership.

advertising a group of activities that involves the presentation of a mass message about a product or an organization; the message is paid for by an identified sponsor.

advocacy advertising a type of promotional advertising designed to support a particular cause, such as the Made In America campaign.

advocate communication channel a promotional method that uses salespersons to contact potential buyers in the target market.

affective the buyer readiness state of a target market in which consumer liking, preference, and conviction is often used to promote existing products.

affordable method a budget technique used to determine promotional expenditures as based on the dollar amount the firm can afford at the moment.

analysis and costing of communication objectives and tasks a method for setting a promotional budget that is determined through examining the expense of individual efforts and the anticipated impact each effort will provide.

assortment the total number of items in the product mix.

basic stock merchandise that remains relatively stable in regard to sales volume and is minimally affected by fashion changes.

behavioral the buyer readiness state of awareness and knowledge that focuses on motivating the consumer to immediately purchase the product.

biogenic buying motive consumer purchasing incentives that relate to physical needs (e.g., food and sex).

branch division the functional division of an organization that is responsible for the multiple units of an organization.

brand a name, term, sign, symbol, design, or combination of them that is intended to identify the goods or services of one seller or group of sellers and to differentiate them from those products of competitors.

brand advertising an advertising effort designed to promote a particular brand.

brand mark the part of a brand that can be recognized, but cannot be vocalized.

brand name the part of a brand that can be vocalized.

breadth a characteristic of an inventory assortment offering a large number of different types of products, but not a large stock of any one style.

break even analysis a method used to determine how much of a product will have to be sold at a certain price in order to cover all the costs.

buyer readiness state used to identify the potential purchasing behavior of an organization's target market.

buying process steps the consumer goes through when deciding what, when, where, and how to buy; includes need recognition, information search, evaluation, purchase decision, and post-purchase behavior.

capital items types of industrial products; goods that partly make up the finished product, such as installations and accessory equipment.

chain store a type of business ownership; multiple retail outlets under common ownership; major functions such as buying, advertising and employment are usually controlled by a central headquarters.

chain operation multiple operations under common ownership whose major functions (e.g., buying, advertising, and human resource management) are often controlled by a central headquarters; the operations handle or carry similar lines of merchandise.

classified advertising advertising that disseminates information about a sale, service, or event.

cognitive a buyer readiness state of awareness and knowledge, commonly used for new product introduction.

competitive-parity method a technique for setting a promotional budget as based on competitors' expenditures.

consistency how closely related the various product lines are in end use, production requirements, and distribution channels.

consumer cooperative association type of business ownership; consumers own shares in the operation. While owners determine business policy, actual operations are maintained by a manager.

content the informational part of a promotional message.

contractual vertical system a marketing channel that consists of independent firms at different levels of production and distribution integrating their programs on retailer cooperatives and franchise organizations.

control division of organization charged with safeguarding the company's financial status; responsibilities include accounting and record keeping, credit and collections, budgeting, and inventory control.

convenience goods those goods the consumer usually purchases frequently, immediately, and with minimum effort in comparison and buying; merchandise the consumer expects to have readily available at a convenient location.

conventional marketing channel traditional distribution arrangement of separate business entities (independent producer, wholesaler, and retailer) that moves the product from the manufacturer to the consumer.

cooperative advertising the manufacturer provides advertising monies to the retailer in exchange for the purchase of goods and name recognition in promotional efforts.

copyright the exclusive right to reproduce, publish, and sell the matter in form of a literary, musical, or artistic work.

corporate vertical system a marketing channel that combines successive stages of production and distribution under a single ownership.

corporation legal form of business organization in which stockholders invest in the company, but do not necessarily share in management decisions. Major decisions are made by a board of directors, while daily operations are conducted by executives and employees of the operation. Stockholders have limited personal responsibility for the firm's debts, as determined by the amount of their investments.

cost factors the variables that are combined to determine the selling price of an item of merchandise.

cost-plus pricing a method of pricing based on the cost of an item with the addition of a dollar amount, usually based on a predetermined mark-up percent.

culture type of market segmentation; inseparable from lifestyle, it refers to the behavior typical of a group or class.

customary pricing a pricing strategy that assumes the customer expects a certain product to be available at a certain price, and that significant deviation in either direction from that customary price will result in decreased demand.

demand pricing a pricing strategy that assumes there is a relationship between the selling price of an item and the amount that can be sold.

demographics refers to the breakdown of the consumer population into statistical categories such as age, gender, education, occupation, income, households, and marital status.

depth characteristic of an inventory assortment offering limited versions of proven popular styles; the number of variants offered within each product of the line.

direct purchasing buying merchandise directly from a source, rather than through a middleman.

direct ratings a method of collecting feedback on types of promotions in which consumers determine the type of advertisement that would influence them to buy the product.

discount terms a manufacturer's reduction in the price of goods offered to the retailer for placement of an order, early payment, quantity purchases, etc.

domestic manufacturers producers that are based and manufacture goods in the United States.

downward vertical communication channel a form of communication that extends from manager to employee.

dual distribution multichannel marketing systems that operate on two different consumer levels; for example, the manufacturer that sells to retail stores and operates its own factory outlet.

durable goods tangible products that normally survive many uses.

economic environment an external influence on business that includes consumer and government spending, consumption, and saving.

emotional appeal promotional effort to induce consumer purchasing that is based on positive or negative feelings (e.g., fear, love, humor, pride, romance, or joy).

emotional buying motive a consumer's intent to purchase a product based on feelings developed without logical thinking (e.g., love and vanity).

employee pilerage losses of merchandise or monies due to theft by the company's personnel.

exclusive distribution strategy a distribution channel alternative that uses a minimal number of retail outlets due to the manufacturer's limited production capacity and due to the product's high-end price point.

exclusivity merchandise that is made available without competition to a specific retailer in a particular trade area.

expert communication channel a form of promotion that presents an individual person with expertise making statements to the target market.

external environment also referred to as the macroenvironment; influences events outside the organization that affect the business; subsets include economic social, political/legal, natural, technological and competetive environments.

fashion goods items popular at a specific time.

foreign manufacturers companies who are headquartered overseas and produce their goods abroad.

formal communication communication within an organization that involves the use of employee handbooks, suggestion systems, newsletters, bulletins, meetings, and education departments.

formal internship program usually offered by a large company, a group of student interns go through preplanned classes and activities to gain exposure to the organization.

format the structure of a promotional message.

franchise type of business ownership; a manufacturer, wholesaler, or service company sells a smaller firm or individual the right to conduct a business in a specified manner within a certain period of time for a fee.

frequency the number of times the message is presented in a promotional effort.

general line wide variety of goods within a product assortment.

hard goods appliances, small electronics, and home furnishings.

high end the upper priced goods within an inventory.

horizontal marketing channel the joining of two or more companies to develop an emerging marketing channel opportunity by contracting on a permanent or temporary basis, or by creating a separate company.

horizontal vertical communication channel communication that flows from manager to manager.

human resource management the personnel division; concerned with hiring, training, motivating, and understanding the needs of employees in order to develop a productive and satisfied work force.

impact the effect or impression that results from the use of a specific media type in a promotional effort.

independently owned a type of business ownership; usually has only one outlet, often owner-managed.

industrial goods the products used to manufacture other products; classified as materials and parts, capital items, or supplies and services.

informal communication the use of vertical and horizontal communication channels for verbal exchange; often referred to as "the grapevine," it reflects unofficial communication.

informal internship program the internship employer and student develop an internship program to meet the employer's needs and the student's academic internship requirements.

institutional advertising advertising designed to build the organization's image and create community goodwill.

intensive distribution strategy a channel design alternative in which the manufacturer's objective is to make the product available to as many different types of retail operations as possible.

information flow directed promotion efforts used to influence product sales from one party to other parties in a marketing channel.

inventory merchandise kept on hand by a manufacturer or retailer.

key vendors the primary manufacturers responsible for the majority of merchandise within the inventory of a retail department.

labeling a part of packaging that consists of printed information describing the product and appearing on the merchandise and/or the package.

layout a floor plan of the internal arrangement of the department with allocated space for each department, as well as nonselling space.

lead time the amount of time required between different receiving stages of the distribution channel; for example, from a manufacturer's perspective, the number of days or weeks between receiving an order and producing those goods or, from a retailer's viewpoint, the number of weeks or months between placing an order with the manufacturer and receiving those goods at the retail operation.

leased department type of business ownership; an arrangement in which a retailer rents space within his/her store to another retailer.

letter of application cover letter; a brief explanation describing the job for which the candidate is applying, the source of the job information, and a summary of the applicant's attributes as they relate to the position.

lifestyles a type of market segmentation; the unique way in which a particular consumer group sets itself apart from others.

limited line a particular type of merchandise assortment (e.g., ladies' career apparel, home accessories, etc.).

loss-leader a product offered at an extremely low price thereby generating no profit and possibly even a loss with the intent of attract customers and building consumer traffic.

loss prevention the activities implemented by an organization to discourage or eliminate shortages, losses due to theft and clerical errors.

low end lower priced merchandise within a product assortment.

macroenvironment *see* external environment.

management a functional department organization in which activities include personnel (human resources), store maintenance, purchasing of supplies and equipment to operate the store, operations, customer services, and business security.

manufacturer/retailer type of business ownership; the manufacturer operates its own retail outlets, eliminating wholesalers and gaining absolute control of the distribution process.

manufacturer's brand *see* national brand.

market positioning arranging for a product to occupy a clear, distinctive, and desirable place in the market and in the minds of consumers.

market segmentation the process of dividing the large consumer population into smaller homogenous sections.

marketing channel arrangement of business entities that moves the product from the manufacturer to the ultimate consumer.

mass media the use of undifferentiated media communication channels for promotional efforts.

materials and parts types of industrial products; goods that enter the manufacturer's product completely, such as raw materials and/or manufactured materials and parts.

Mazur Plan a concept developed to organize store departmentalization by functions; merchandising, publicity, management, and control.

merchandising an operational division that includes responsibility for all activities involved in buying and selling merchandise.

mission statement a document that provides guidance to create a shared sense of direction, opportunity, significance, and achievement for an organization's executives and employees.

moral appeal a promotional effort that reflects an audience's sense of what is right and wrong.

multichannel marketing system a marketing channel that usually combines several styles of retailing with an integration of some distribution and management functions.

national brand a manufacturer's brand that is available nationwide.

natural environment an external influence on business that encompasses the natural elements such as wind, water, and soil.

nondurable goods tangible goods that are normally consumed in one or few uses.

nonpersonal communication channel the types of promotional efforts that utilize mass and specialized media to reach a wide range of consumers.

nonstore selling an alternative channel of distribution that does not require a physical plant; examples include direct selling, party plans, mail order retailing, catalogue retailing, telephone, television selling, and electronic retailing (including computer selling).

operations management a functional division that includes receiving, marking, checking of merchandise receipts; warehouse distribution; and shipping of merchandise.

opinion leader a term used to identify types of consumers; the member of a reference group who exerts influence over consumer decision-making by colleagues within a reference group.

order processing part of physical distribution; how orders are handled.

ownership group type of business ownership; a parent corporation owns divisions of retail institutions.

packaging the activities of designing and producing the container or wrapper for a product.

partnership legal form of business organization; two or more persons invest their time and money while maintaining liability for business debts.

patronage buying motive reasons why consumers choose one place to shop rather than another.

payment flow method(s) used by marketing channel members to pay their bills; also includes the parties to whom the payments are made.

penetration pricing a pricing strategy that is designed to capture a large mass market by offering the product at a low price.

percentage of sales method a technique for setting the promotional budget that is based on the organization's sales volume.

personal communication channel a type of promotion that involves direct people-to-people communication; types include advocate, expert and social.

personal selling includes wholesale selling or contact selling, since the seller usually contacts the customer; also includes retail selling where the customer usually approaches the retail operation.

personnel the employees of an organization.

physical distribution involves the tasks of planning, implementing, and controlling the physical flows of raw materials and final goods from points of origin to points of use to meet the needs of customers at a profit.

physical flow movement of the actual product from raw materials to end users.

political/legal environment an external influence on organizations that includes political and governmental issues such as import quotas, trade restrictions, and business regulations.

portfolio tests a method of collecting feedback on types of promotions in which a group of consumers analyzes an assortment of advertisements and then is tested for recall and recognition.

prestige pricing a pricing strategy that assumes the customer infers a relationship between price and quality and will not buy a product if the price is too low.

price skimming a pricing strategy which says that the price for something will be higher than normal in an attempt to generate a large sales volume early before competition has a chance to get in and drive prices down.

private brand a brand name owned by a middleman, distributor or dealer.

private label a brand name that is exclusive to the distributor.

private label source a manufacturer producing merchandise under a label other than its own name.

product anything offered to a market for attention, acquisition, use, or consumption; capable of satisfying a consumer's want or need and may be an object, a service, an activity, a person, a place, an organization, or an idea.

product life cycle the time period during which a particular item, classification, color, or style will sell well enough to generate a profit.

product assortment *see* product mix.

product line a group of products that are closely related, either because they function in a similar manner, are sold to the same customer groups, are marketed through the same types of outlets, or fall within given price ranges.

product mix the set of all products that a particular seller offers for sale to buyers; also referred to as the product assortment.

promotional pricing a method of pricing merchandise so that the retail price implies a value or bargain to the consumer.

promotion budget the total amount of funds to be spent on promotional efforts and the allocation of these funds to individual public relations activities.

promotional sources manufacturers providing merchandise that can be sold as special purchase or value items at promotional prices.

psychogenic buying motive a consumer buying incentive that stems from psychological needs (e.g., to enhance the ego or to protect).

psychological pricing a pricing strategy that uses odd-numbered endings to imply sale pricing (e.g., $7.99 and $11.95).

public relations concerned with all nonpersonal selling activities including sales promotions, advertising, and special events; utilized to project the character and image of the organization.

rate method a method of pricing products that includes a standard initial markup, such as simply doubling the cost of a product to determine the retail price.

rational appeal promotional effort that stresses self-interest by showing that the product will produce claimed benefits; a promotional appeal based on logic and knowledge.

rational buying motive purchasing incentive for consumers that involves judgment and logical thinking (e.g., security and durability).

reach the number of persons communicated with by a certain media type in a specific target market.

reference groups type of market segmentation that analyzes those consumers who are influential in shaping the attitudes and opinions of others.

regional markets trade markets located in geographical areas across the country, such as Kansas City, Chicago, and San Francisco.

regular-priced sources manufacturers providing merchandise that the retail buyer sells at a nonsale price.

resident buying office a company that the retail organization pays a fee in exchange for consultion about merchandise selection and a variety of services such as direct mail, private label, and quantity purchases; an outside agency whose primary responsibility and specialization is coverage of the various merchandise classifications it represents.

resume a brief account of one's professional or work experience and education, often submitted with a letter of application.

sale advertising advertising designed to announce specific value items.

sales promotion any promotional activity other than advertising, publicity, and personal selling that attracts the public to an organization, stimulates purchasing, and makes a profit for that organization.

sample line a representation of styles within a manufacturer's seasonal line used by manufacturer's representative to show to the retail store buyer.

selective distribution strategy a distribution channel design alternative in which the manufacturer sells the product line to a somewhat limited number or type of outlets.

selective media specialized print, electronic, or display methods used for promotional efforts.

secondary vendors manufacturers that are carried in lesser amount than key vendors within a retailer's inventory.

service an intangible product offered for sale such as activity, idea, benefit or satisfaction.

shopping goods merchandise that the consumer usually compares on basis of quality, price, and style.

shortage the financial difference between an organization's book inventory and physical inventory; also referred to as shrinkage.

shrinkage *see* shortage.

soft goods textiles and apparel products.

social classes type of market segmentation; homogeneous divisions of families and individuals within a society determined by occupation, source of income, education, family background, dwelling type, and other variables.

social communication channel word-of-mouth communication among neighbors, family, friends, and associates.

social environment an external influence on businesses that includes social attitudes and changes such as population shifts, attitudes about behaviors, and geographical residence patterns.

sole proprietorship legal form of business organization; one person owns the business and assumes personal responsibility for its debts.

source credibility media effort that attempts to establish expertise, trustworthiness, and likability.

specialty goods products with unique characteristics and/or brand identification for which a significant group of consumers is habitually willing to make a special buying effort.

staple goods items constantly in demand and minimally influenced by fashion changes.

structure the format of a promotional message.

supplies and services types of industrial goods; items that do not enter the finished product in any form, such as operating supplies and maintenance and repair items, maintenance and repair services, and business advisory services.

target market the group of consumers to whom a particular organization is aiming their product.

technological environment an external influence that affects business; technological influences include computers, manufacturing equipment, newly developed textiles, and related products.

title flow the passage of ownership of a product from one marketing organization to another.

trade shows the market exhibitions by a substantial number of manufacturers' representatives who show and sell their seasonal product lines to retail buyers.

trademark a brand or part of a brand that is given legal protection because it is capable of exclusive rights.

transportation the physical distribution of merchandise; how products are shipped.

uncontrollable variables the external influences of social, technological, natural, and economic environments that affect an organization, but which the organization cannot readily manipulate.

unsought goods a customer may or may not know about these products, does not normally think of buying them; but may be made aware of the product through advertising.

upward vertical communication channel an employee to manager form of communication.

vertical marketing channel producer(s), wholesaler(s), and retailer(s) are cooperating as a unified group to move product from manufacturer to consumer.

warehousing an aspect of physical distribution; where inventory is located.

Index

Academic advisors. See *Faculty*.
Advertising, 115, 149, 151, 154–156, 159. See also *Promotion*.
  cooperative, 154
  types of, 155–159
Alumni, 3, 10, 63
Ancillary services, 192
Apparel manufacturing firms, 10–11, 65, 95, 110–111, 123, 189
  application for, 17–22
Apparel marts, 11
Avon, 125

Bait and switch, 130
Bill Blass, 156
Budgeting, 64
Buyer. See *Customer*.

Careers
  ancillary services, 192
  buyers, 74, 112, 123, 152, 191
  fashion designer, 190–191
  manufacturers representative, 74, 112, 155
  merchandise coordinator, 192
  options, 189–192
  planning, 4
  retailer, 191–192
  visual merchandising, 159, 192
Channels, marketing. See *Marketing*.
Chic Jeans, 155
Companies. See also *Organization of businesses*.
  competitors, 101–105, 118, 122, 130, 154
  customer service department, 124–125

evaluation of, 179–188
goals, 99–100
market positioning, 100–101
mission statement, 97–99
organization of, 68–89
personality of, 82–83
pricing. See *Pricing*.
Computers, 111–112
Cotton Council, 129, 154
Culture, 94
Customer
buyer readiness, 149
buying motives, 91–95, 149–150.
decision making, 92–93
lifestyles, 94–95
needs, 91
reference groups, 94–95
service, 121–127

Daily News Record, 10
Demographics, 93–94, 109
Dillard's, 44
Distribution, 108, 141–148
Donegar and Associates, 123
DuPont, 123, 190

Earnshaw's, 10
Employers, 1, 10–12
researching, 1, 7
Employee theft, 72–73
Escada, 145
Esprit, 64, 144, 151
External environment, 107–112
economic, 108
natural, 110–111
political/legal, 110
social, 109
technological, 111–112

Faculty, 10, 26, 62
Fairchild's Directory, 3, 10
Fashion designers, 190–191
Fashion Group International, 11, 99
Franchise, 68–69, 143
Halls Merchandising, 2, 44

Hanes Hosiery, 145
Housing, 49, 63
Human resources. See *Organization of businesses.*

International Textile and Apparel Associations (ITAA), 10
Internships
    agreement for, 161–162
    changing, 62
    creating, 2
    evaluation, 63, 179–188
    formal, 44
    informal, 44
    paid/unpaid, 2
    planning for, 1
    time line for, 3
    Weekly Activity Report Forms, 163–178
Interviews, 44–51
    follow-up letter, 52–55
    questions asked during interview, 48–51
Inventory, 71, 74, 146, 148

Jobs
    application forms, 13–22
    attitudes about, 58
    changing, 62
    evaluation by employer, 181–183
    interviewing for, see *Interviews*
    letter of application for, 38 – 43
    on-the-job expectations, 57– 63
    rules for workplace, 61
    searching for, 5–9
    tips for success, 61–62
    work habits, 60–62
Jones Store Company, 156

Kansas City Star, 156
K-Mart, 150, 154

Letter of application, 38 – 43
    structure of, 39 – 40
Liz Claiborne, 125, 145
Loss prevention, 72–73

Macroenvironment, see *External environment.*
Macy's, 44

Manufacturers representative, 74–75, 79
Marketing, 100, 141–160. See also *Distribution* and *Promotion*.
  channel design, 145–146
  channel flows, 142–143
  channels, 141–148
  conventional channel, 141–142
  evaluation of, 180
  horizontal channel, 144
  media, use of, 153
  multichannel, 144
  vertical channel, 143–144
  visual, 159
Markets
  positioning, 100–101
  repositioning, 100–101
  segmentation, 93
Mazur, Paul, 71
Merchandise
  mass, 145
  mix, 75
  sources of, 75
  unsold, 140
Milliken, 152

National Retail Federation, 71
Neiman Marcus, 152
Networking, 10, 62, 99
  sample letter for, 12
Nordstrom, 98

Organization of businesses, 67–89
  chain operations, 68
  communication channels, 89
  consumer cooperative association, 69
  control, 68, 71, 81–82
  departmentalization, 71–72
  franchise, 68–69, 143
  legal forms, 68
  merchandizing, 71, 74–77
  operations, 72–74
  ownership of, 68–69
  ownership group, 68
  personnel, 71, 78–81
  public relations, 71, 82–84
Pay-Less Shoes, 123

Pinstripe Petites, 101
Pricing, 129–142
  "bait and switch," 130
  cost-plus, 131
  decisions, 130
  demand, 131
  garment costing sheet, 134–138
  penetration, 131
  promotional, 131
  skimming, 131
  strategies, 133
  timing calendar, 141
Products
  branding, 118–119
  classification, 114–118
  distribution. See *Distribution.*
  durable, 115
  identification, 113–120
  levels, 113–114
  line, 125–127
  mix, 75, 125–127
  nondurable, 114
  packaging, 119–120
  services, 115
  success requirements, 179
Promotion, 71, 75, 82, 149–160. See also *Marketing.*
  budget for, 154
  communication channels, 151–152
  displays, 159
  feedback, 159–160
  media, use of, 153
  message, 150–151
  target markets, 149–150
Public relations. See *Organization of businesses.*

Ralph Lauren, 190
References, 26
Retail, 189, 191
  application forms for, 15–16
Resumes, 13, 23–38
  do's and don'ts, 37–38
  key components of, 37
  organizational worksheet for, 28–30
  power words in, 31–33
Revlon, 154

Saks Fifth Avenue, 2, 44
Sales, 111, 131, 149, 154. See also *Promotion.*
  non-store selling, 67, 70
Sam's Wholesale Club, 121
Sears, Roebuck, and Co., 100
Services, 70–71
Sheldon's Retail Directory, 3, 10
Shrinkage, 72
Standard & Poor, 3, 10
Stores, 3, 10

Timing calendar. See *Pricing.*
Transportation, 64

U.S. Timex, 145

Vanity Fair, 123
Visual merchandising, 192

Wall Street Journal, 10
Weekly Activity Report Forms, 163–178
Women's Network Organization, 98
Women's Wear Daily, 3, 10
Wool Bureau, 129, 154